# HOW TO TREAT
# DIFFERENT TYPES OF CHURCH MEMBERS

## JACK HYLES

# How to Treat
# Different Types of Church Members

By Jack Hyles

# Contents

# Introduction

Pastors who leave churches because of problems, find the same problems welcoming them on the front porch of their new pastorate.

Pastors who leave churches because of disgruntled members, will find those same members waiting for them at the door of their new church.

Pastors who leave churches because of an enemy, will find that same enemy is a member of the church where they are going.

One cannot run from problems concerning human relationships. These problems must not be avoided or evaded; they must be solved. Life is composed of a series of human relationships. Much of one's success in life depends upon the proper handling of these relationships and the proper priorities concerning them.

Whether we like it or not, we must relate to people who are weaker than we are. Whether we like it or not, we must learn to relate to people who are stronger than we are. Whether we like it or not, we must learn to relate to our enemies, to the fallen, to the tormentor and to the tempter. All of these are found in every church, and the members of every church must learn to face them properly if we are to reach a lost world.

I have preached all over this great nation. I have delivered over 45,500 sermons. I have found that God's people are basically the same everywhere. Every little group of us is a microcosm of all of us, and each of us must learn to live peaceably with the rest of us. To that end, I give you this book and my heart.

# Chapter 1

# Treatment of Those
# With Whom You Disagree

Romans 12:10, "Be kindly affectioned one to another with brotherly love; in honour preferring one another."

Ephesians 4:1-3, "I therefore, the prisoner of the Lord, beseech you that ye walk worthy of the vocation wherewith ye are called, with all lowliness and meekness, with longsuffering, forbearing one another in love; endeavouring to keep the unity of the Spirit in the bond of peace."

Ephesians 4:30-32, "And grieve not the Holy Spirit of God, whereby ye are sealed unto the day of redemption. Let all bitterness, and wrath, and anger, and clamour, and evil speaking, be put away from you, with all malice: and be ye kind one to another, tenderhearted, forgiving one another, even as God for Christ's sake hath forgiven you."

I Corinthians 6:7, "Now therefore there is utterly a fault among you, because ye go to law one with another. Why do ye not rather take wrong? why do ye not rather suffer yourselves to be defrauded?"

As is said often in this manuscript, the modern fundamental church is far more intricate than it was in previous generations. In earlier times church members were together only a few hours a week. On Sunday morning we met for Sunday school, which was followed by the morning preaching service. About half of us returned on Sunday night, and a remnant came to the midweek service on Wednesday evening. Because of this, we did not know

3

each other real well, and the possibilities of irritation were few and seldom. We could wear our best behavior for an hour or two. So, it was easy to like each other.

The modern fundamental church is far more complicated than that. We are together often and for long periods at a time. For example, the First Baptist Church of Hammond has many things for our children and young people. We have our Christian schools where a child can enroll in kindergarten at the age of 4 and 19 years later graduate from our college with his master's degree. This means that we are together at school five days a week for seven or eight hours. Included in the school program are many extra-curricular activities such as sports, cheerleading, pep squads, shops, class meetings, class parties, field trips, etc. Then the church provides regular youth activities, camps, choirs, children's clubs and intramural boys baseball league, Bible studies, prayer groups, teenage soul winning, high school Bible clubs, etc.

This means that the fundamental church of today has become its own little community. We are together not only for two or three hours on Sunday, but we are together every day of the week.

These activities cause multitudes of opportunities for interaction and provide many different forms of relationships. The average parent, for example, has regular contact with those who lead his children. There are many of these such as the principal, the teachers, the coaches, the choir directors, the youth directors, the Sunday school teachers, the Bible club leaders, the soul-winning captains and many others. We no longer simply see each other sitting side by side in the quietness of a morning service, but we are constantly interacting with church people. We see each other as we are. We see faults as well as strengths, liabilities as well as assets, and the minus as well as the plus.

Then, when we go to church, we may share the same Sunday school class with the parents of the child we teach in school and with the teacher of our child. We may sit in the same choir with them or usher side by side with them. We may sit with them in the same Sunday school class or share the same bus route. We may sit side by side in one of many other church activities of the modern fundamental church. All of this means that there are more chances for disagreement, irritability and even strife. Constant care must be taken in order to minimize friction caused by disagreements.

1. *Do not express disappointments.* So much can be left unsaid. Never use such statements as, "I am disappointed with you," "I am disappointed in him," or "I wish you had not done that." There is no law that says that we must comment on everything that is said to us or that we must critique everything that is done to us. If something has been done that has disappointed us, it has already been done and there is no undoing it. There is no need for us to summarize our displeasure. This is the time to use the art of silence.

2. *Do not give your opinions if not asked or if they are outside your area of authority.* There is no law that requires us to always give an opinion, and it is usually best to keep our opinions to ourselves unless our advice is requested or unless it is within our area of authority and responsibility. If someone expresses an opinion with which we disagree, it is usually best not to voice that disagreement.

An aid to this is the division of responsibilities. I am a firm believer in delegation and separation of authority. The more decisions that we share, the more opportunities we create for disagreement. For example, in a home I think it is wise for the husband and wife to divide responsibilities, therefore making as few decisions together as possible. For example, at our house I take care of the finances. That is my responsibility and my area. For these many years I have given Mrs. Hyles an allowance every week from whence she buys groceries and incidentals and then has some left for herself. She spends this money as she chooses. Apart from that, I am in charge of the rest of the finances. We never have to argue or fuss about money. She has her area of responsibility and I have mine.

On the other hand, the house, its furnishing and keeping are her responsibilities. She chooses where the furniture is placed, and all the decisions concerning the house are hers. If I come in some night and the sofa is in the entrance hall blocking the door, I will simply crawl over the sofa and say, "What a novel idea! Not many wives realize how tired their husbands are and are thoughtful enough to give him a place to rest as soon as he walks in the door."

Other responsibilities are divided likewise, which means there is no opportunity to disagree or argue. This is why I advise young couples not to go grocery shopping together. She may want one brand; he may want another. If 100 objects are bought together, then there are 100 opportunities for disagreement. I recommend that if young couples *do* go grocery shopping together, that one should simply push the cart and the other make all the decisions. These are just illustrations in suggesting that we divide responsibilities so as to avoid disagreement opportunities.

This same thing should be applied at church. There is no need to appoint five people on a flower committee to spend seven days deciding what flowers are going to be on the communion table on Sunday morning. Let one person do it and avoid chances for disagreement. There is no need for a music committee to decide what the choir special will be on Sunday. Let the music director decide. Delegate responsibility. Give authority. Divide the decision-making processes. There is no need for a youth committee to plan the youth activity. Let the youth director do it. Let the Christian school teacher be the school teacher. Let the principal be the principal. Let the choir director be the choir director. Let the bus director be the bus director. Let the head usher be the head usher. Choose qualified, spiritual, amiable people and give them each an area of responsibility. Of course, there should be veto power at the top, but this power should be used wisely, carefully and seldom. Of course, it must be remembered that the responsibility is delegated, but let there be responsibility. This gives us less opportunity to express unnecessary opinions that could cause strife and friction.

If the wife asks the husband what he thinks about her new hairdo, he can sidestep the answer graciously by saying, "You always look attractive." This policy can be applied to all the areas of our family and church life and will keep our disagreements from surfacing, and believe me, most of them do not need to surface!

Of course, the wise person will seek counsel from others concerning the decisions that he must make within his sphere of authority, but until such advice is sought, silence is usually the best course of action.

3. *Do not demand your area of authority.* There are some fields and areas in which one might be more qualified than the person to whom this responsibility has been delegated. Then, there are some people who will give you advice that is unwanted and that you think is not needed. In other words, they are not complying with the suggestions made in the previous point. When such intrusion is made, do not bristle; do not remind them that they are out of bounds; listen to them patiently without making rebuttal; thank them kindly for their advice; and then choose yourself whether or not to use it. Do not let them know who is boss or remind them of their intrusion. Do not flaunt your title, your power or your position. Simply realize that the power of decision is in your hands, and if someone has unwisely used his right to intrude, his intrusion makes you no less responsible to make the decision. Because of this, there is no need for rebuttal on your part. Simply listen to the one who is out of order, thank him for his suggestion and go about your business of making the right decision within the sphere of your responsibility.

4. *Do not start an answer with a negative comment.* Such statements as, "I don't agree," "You're wrong," etc., should never precede a statement of disagreement. It would be far better to use such statements as, "What do you think about this additional thought?" "Here is an idea along the same line," or "Your statement has led me to this thought."

When someone presents an idea with which we do not agree, negative statements at the first of our reply are like a slap in the face and can partially or totally close the door of their acceptance of our idea which is about to be expressed.

5. *Allow the other person to have at least a possibility of being right, or the possibility that he may be partially right, or the possibility that some of his opinions may be right.* Leave him room to breathe. Leave him with some dignity.

Recently a young lady was expelled from Hyles-Anderson College. Shortly after this expulsion, I was in her home church preaching for two days. I asked her father if he and his daughter would have lunch with me on Tuesday. The young lady was not treated as a criminal. She was treated with dignity and propriety. Toward the end of the conversation I told her that there was a possibility that we too had made some mistakes. I asked her to tell me frankly of any area in our college where she thought we could improve and where students could be treated with more justice, propriety and discernment. Though she was reluctant to do so, upon my insistence, she did. Her suggestions were very helpful, and some of them are being implemented at this time at Hyles-Anderson College. Our conversation was a help to me and a help to her. She was a fine young lady who had made some mistakes and who wanted to correct them. I did her a service by giving her a chance to help us, and she did us a service by her willingness to help. I predict that she will return to us and that she will be a cooperative, obedient and diligent student; and, by the way, she and I will no doubt be friends for life.

Fundamentalists believe strongly, and this is good, but in our interaction with each other, we must not always feel that there is no possibility of our making a mistake. We must remember that honest disagreement is not always rebellion or anarchy.

6. *Do not express your opinion unless you have the power to help.* If someone asks me after a certain course of action has been taken, "Did I do right?" I do not reply. The act has been committed, and it is too late for advice. I am always happy to give advice and counsel when asked, but I do not volunteer that advice nor do I expose my opinion when it can plant a seed that could lead to disagreement and perhaps strife.

7. *Do not express your opinion when you are aware of the advice that has been given by your peers whom you respect and with whom you work.*

Just the night before the writing of this chapter, a Hyles-Anderson College student came to my office asking my advice about a matter. He reminded me that he had already sought advice from Dr.

Evans, the President of Hyles-Anderson College, and then told me quickly the advice that Dr. Evans had given him. I graciously declined to give him advice because I did not want to nullify or conflict with the counsel given him by Dr. Evans, whom I respect tremendously.

This is not to say that the young person should not have sought advice from more than one, and I would certainly have counseled with him and advised him had I not known of his previous approach to Dr. Evans, or if I had not known the nature of Dr. Evans' advice.

8. *Ask yourself, "Who probably has the best chance of being right on this issue?"* If the administrative committee of Hyles-Anderson College is discussing college curriculum concerning history classes, I would think that Dr. Evans, one of fundamentalism's outstanding historians, would be eminently more qualified than I. So, if he and I were to disagree concerning history curriculum, I would probably yield to his position. If we then turned to the subject of the curriculum of pastoral theology and had a disagreement, Dr. Evans would no doubt yield to my position. Such action should also be considered when the parent disagrees with the teacher concerning a school matter, when the teacher disagrees with the principal concerning administration, when the member of the church disagrees with the pastor concerning his preaching and many other areas of the church program.

I am an opinionated person; most leaders are. However, I realize that my knowledge of music is very limited. To be sure, there are boundaries that I build around the music program at First Baptist Church and that of Hyles-Anderson College, but within those boundaries, I almost always yield to the wishes and decisions of those in charge of the music departments. Of course, those who lead these departments are lovely people and would bow to my wishes on any occasion. I accept the right to have this authority and to exercise it if I see fit, but the possession of this right does not necessitate its frequent use. It must be remembered that we have as much a right not to use our rights as we have to use them. We should not abuse them by unwise use or an excess of frequency.

9. *If someone refutes your opinion, let it stop there.* There is no need for rebuttal. Simply voice your willingness to consider the opinion that has been expressed and courteously refrain from expressing yours.

For years I have had a little hobby—that of trying to improve the disposition of disagreeable people. It is a wonderful little game that I play, and it is among my favorite hobbies. I was in a southern city returning a rented car. It was very early in the morning—probably an hour before sunrise. I went to the counter to return my papers and keys. I greeted the young lady behind the counter wih "Good morning! How are you today?" She gave no reply; in fact, she didn't even look up. She simply took the papers and the keys and began her routine immediately. I wanted to help her get in a good mood, so I started my little game of trying to make her happy. Again I said, "Good morning! How are things going today?" Again there was no reply. Similar further attempts were made to brighten her day, and all ended in failure. I then leaned over the counter, looked up at her and said, "Why are you mad at me?"

She grinned and replied, "Mister, it's too early to be nice!"

I said to her, "Ma'am, it's just as early on this side of the counter as it is on that side of the counter."

She then began to laugh and thanked me for brightening her morning. We both went on our way rejoicing.

Several years ago I was in a small city in southern Louisiana. The dear pastor took me to lunch on Tuesday. He chose a little downtown restaurant, locally operated and obviously very popular. The waitress came to take our order. She was a little bit less than kind. (Ah, here was another splendid chance for me to practice my hobby!) The pastor ordered first, and then it was my time. I looked up with a smile and said, "I'll take a Big Mac, French fries and a chocolate shake." (We were not at McDonald's.) She looked at me sternly, then smiled and said, "Mister, a Big Mac sure beats anything we have to serve here!" I found that she was angry at her employer, and as I remember, she had decided to quit her job. When she replied that a Big Mac was better than their food, all of us laughed. My mission was accomplished! Well, nearly, for before I left the restaurant, it was my joy to lead her to Jesus Christ!

I was on an airplane flying to the Greensboro - High Point - Winston-Salem Airport. I sat down beside a gentleman—well, at least I thought he would be a gentleman. I spoke to him. He did not reply. I spoke again. There was no answer. (Ah, ha! Here is a chance for me to enjoy my hobby of cheering up a fellow human being.) I proceeded with such statements and questions as, "Isn't it a nice day?" etc. All of my attempts to gain a response failed. I then tapped him on the shoulder. He looked at me and I started using my hands as if I were speaking to him in the sign language. With a puzzled look on his face he asked, "Fellow, what are you doing?"

I said, "Sir, I thought perhaps you were deaf since you had not replied to any of my questions or statements, so I was trying to communicate in the sign language." He began to laugh immediately, shook my hand and introduced himself. This gave me a chance to witness to him and to lead him to Christ. (Again, mission accomplished and hobby enjoyed!)

I was flying from Orlando, Florida, to Chicago. I had a change of planes in Tampa, Florida. Upon landing at the Tampa airport I found that my next flight would be three hours late. There are few places in the world more boring for three hours than an airport, so I went to the restaurant upstairs and was met at the entrance by a young waitress. She asked if I wanted a booth. I replied, "Yes, ma'am."

She led me to a booth and said, "Is this all right?"

I said, "Yes, ma'am."

She came back in a few minutes and said, "Sir, are you ready to order?"

I said, "Yes, ma'am."

She took her little order pad, threw it on the table in front of me, put her hands on her hips, and said in a gruff voice, "Yes, ma'am! Yes, ma'am! Yes, ma'am! Yes, ma'am! Yes, ma'am! Yes, ma'am! Yes, ma'am! Yes, ma'am! Don't you know any words, sir, other than 'Yes, ma'am'?"

I replied, "Yes, ma'am."

She turned and walked away abruptly upon receiving my order. When she came back she tossed my plate on the table, causing some of the food to spill. (Hey, here's a chance to do my hobby, but believe me, this one was a real challenge!) When she returned to give me my ticket, she turned her back, faced the other way and wrote my check. She then handed it behind her back to me and walked away angrily. I had had a light lunch; in fact, my ticket was only $1.67. As I left, I placed a $5 bill on the table and slowly walked toward the cash register. While I was paying my bill of $1.67, the little waitress came walking up and said abruptly, "Mister, you dropped some money on the table as you left," and handed me the $5 bill. I returned it to her saying, "Don't they tip in Tampa?" She broke! Tears filled her eyes and she asked, "Mister, did you leave me a $5 tip after I've been so rude to you?"

I said to her, "Young lady, you're not a bad person. You have a heartache. There is a reason why you were unkind to me, and I do not feel in any way negative about you." She continued to cry in that busy little restaurant filled with people, and she told me a sad story. Her husband had left her a few days before. She had had to get a job and the salary was not large enough to care for the children that he had left with her. She told me that she didn't want to live! Standing there in the busy restaurant, right at the entrance, I led her to Jesus Christ. Then she apologized for having been rude to me. (Praise the Lord! Mission accomplished! Mission more than accomplished; what a nice hobby!) A couple of hours later I was walking toward my airplane, and whom did I meet but this little waitress! I smiled and said, "Are you still saved?"

She shyly responded, through an impish grin, "Yes, ma'am!"

For years I have been trading at a little convenience, drive-in market called The White Hen Pantry. It is located just a few blocks from where I live, and it is convenient for me to stop by every morning on the way to work to purchase a USA TODAY newspaper, and occasionally I will make other purchases. One day an older lady who often waited on me there asked me, "What's wrong with you today?"

I replied, "Nothing. Why do you ask?"

She said, "This is the first time that you have ever been in here through these years without whistling or singing. There must be something wrong." She seemed a little sad and nearly out-of-sorts. (I immediately saw another opportunity to use my hobby.) I told her that nothing was wrong.

She said, "Then why do you always sing and whistle?"

I said, "Because I am happy."

She said, "In this old sick world, how can you be happy?" I looked around and saw that there were no other customers there. This in itself was a miracle. I think the Lord dispatched an angel out in the street, telling folks to drive on by for awhile. For some time no one came in the store, giving me a chance to tell her why I am happy and to share with her that happiness. In a few moments she received the Author of that happiness as her Saviour. (Once again—mission accomplished! Hobby enjoyed!)

Several years passed. One day I was requested to go visit a man who was very ill. He had asked for me. When I got to the house he told me why he wanted to see me. The lady whom I had won to Christ at The White Hen Pantry was his wife. I did not know it, but she had passed away not long before my visit with him, and he wanted to thank me for being so nice to his wife and to tell me how much she loved and appreciated me. I sat there with him on a Sunday afternoon and won him to Christ. Ah, hobbies have bonuses, don't they?

The Christian should always be working toward harmony. Needless disagreements should be circumvented and avoided if at all possible. Most of our disagreements are so useless and needless, and so in our fundamental churches where we are so interwoven and have so much interaction, we need to be on constant guard to prevent them.

I love good music. Nearly every day of my life I take time to listen to classical music. I do not allow this kind of music to be used in our church because I believe that church music should be limited to hymns and Gospel songs, but in my personal life I often drive or eat with the classics as background music. The reason I love good music is because good music is harmony of sound, and I want to dwell in harmony, which leads me to choose sound that is harmonious. This is one reason (among many) that rock music is wrong. It is sound with disharmony.

I love good literature, especially good poetry. I read it regularly and I write it often. Poetry is harmony of words and meter. Bad literature is words with disharmony. Good literature promotes harmony and is harmony.

I love good art; in fact, I often visit art galeries. I do this because good art is harmony of colors. Modern art, which often looks like someone has taken a canvas, squirted ketchup on it, thrown three raw eggs at it and stirred them with a touch of mustard, framed it and called it art—this is disharmony of color, whereas good art is harmony of color.

My favorite subject in school was algebra, because in algebra the balancing of the equation is the bringing of harmony. Here we have a harmony of numbers. Basically harmony is balancing life's equations.

I was staying in a hotel in Milford, Ohio. My room was on the fifth floor. As I got off the elevator, I was facing a wall. On that wall was a painting. That painting was crooked. I can't stand a crooked painting, so I straightened it. I went to my room, unpacked my bags and decided to go to the restaurant for a bowl of soup. While I was waiting for the elevator, I turned and looked at the painting. It was crooked again. I straightened it. I went down to the restaurant, ate a bowl of soup, came back up to the fifth floor. As I got off the elevator, I noticed the painting was crooked again. I straightened it. I went to my room, washed, brushed my teeth, got my Bible, went to the lobby where I was to be met and driven to the services. As I was waiting for the elevator, I noticed the painting was crooked again. I straightened it. I went to the church, preached, and was driven back to the hotel. When I got off the elevator, I noticed the painting was crooked again. I straightened it. I went to my room, went to bed, but I couldn't sleep. All I could think about was, "Is that painting crooked again?" I got out of bed, put on my pants and shirt over my pajamas, walked down the hallway to see if the painting was crooked or straight. It was crooked. I got on the elevator and went downstairs, walked to the desk and asked the night clerk if she had someone who could come up and straighten the painting on the fifth floor. She said that the maintenance men were all off for the evening and that there was no one who could do it. I asked her if she had a hammer and nails. She said she did. I said, "Would you let me borrow them so I can straighten that painting permanently?"

She said, "Sir, why do you want that painting straight?"

"Because I can't sleep!" I said.

She smiled and gave me a hammer and a nail. I went upstairs, straightened the painting, returned the hammer, returned to my room and got a good night's sleep. All was harmonious again.

I cannot stand needless disharmony. Complaining affects me like a shovel being scraped against concrete. I try not to practice it, and I try not to be around people who do. It promotes disharmony and an unbalanced equation.

This is the reason that I do not go out to eat after services. I cannot be around the criticism of God's people by God's people. I simply refuse to listen to negatives. I do not want this computer on top of my shoulders called a mind to be programmed with negatives. I have people who need me to lift them, to comfort them, to proclaim victory to them, and I cannot do it if I live amidst talk that is not harmonious and if I program my computer with negatives.

A fundamental church should be a refuge, a haven, a pavilion, a shelter from the irritability of our critique-infested society. If, in fact, a church is exactly this, its members must learn to live with their disagreements which, because we are human, will exist. If because we are Christians we can refrain from expressing disappointment of people; refrain from giving opinions that are not requested; refrain from fighting for our rights and our areas of authority; refrain from negative statements such as, "I don't agree!" or "You're wrong on that!" and allow each other to have the possibility of being at least partially right; refrain from expressing our opinions unless they will help; ask ourselves, "Who probably has the best chance of being right here?" and refrain from responding when our opinion is refuted, we will have made at least some progress toward harmony and peace!

Don't forget our little hobby—that delightful little game of balancing human equations and promoting harmony between ourselves and those whom the will of God has brought close to us—often on a daily basis—and with whom the Holy Spirit has led us to interact. May that same Holy Spirit lead us to interact in such a way so as to treat properly and with grace those with whom we disagree.

# Chapter 2

# Treatment of the Fallen

Galatians 6:1, "Brethren, if a man be overtaken in a fault, ye which are spiritual, restore such an one in the spirit of meekness; considering thyself, lest thou also be tempted."

Galatians 5:19-24, "Now the works of the flesh are manifest, which are these; Adultery, fornication, uncleanness, lasciviousness, idolatry, witchcraft, hatred, variance, emulations, wrath, strife, seditions, heresies, envyings, murders, drunkenness, revellings, and such like: of the which I tell you before, as I have also told you in time past, that they which do such things shall not inherit the kingdom of God. But the fruit of the Spirit is love, joy, peace, longsuffering, gentleness, goodness, faith, meekness, temperance: against such there is no law. And they that are Christ's have crucified the flesh with the affections and lusts."

In order to fully understand Galatians 6:1, one must connect it with Galatians 5:19-24. The one overtaken in a fault in Galatians 6:1 is no doubt one overtaken in one of the faults mentioned in Galatians 5:19-21. The one who is spiritual in Galatians 6:1 is the one who possesses the fruit of the Spirit in Galatians 5:22, 23. In other words, when the one who has the fruit of the Spirit overtakes one who has the works of the flesh in committing one of these works, he receives instructions in Galatians 6:1 as to what he is to do. Care must be taken that one who commits some of the works of the flesh does not take it upon himself to correct one who commits others of the works of the flesh. In other words, the one who is guilty of wrath is not qualified to lift the one who is guilty of fornication. One who is guilty of strife is not qualified to lift the one who is guilty of lasciviousness. In such a case the blind leads the blind, the fallen lifts the fallen, and the flesh attempts to make the flesh spiritual, which, of course, is impossible.

We must be careful, therefore, to address Galatians 6:1 only to the spiritual, to those who walk according to the fruit of the Spirit, as listed in Galatians 5:22, 23, and do not walk according to any of the works of the flesh as listed in Galatians 5:19-21.

1. *The word, "overtaken," implies a witness.* When someone who is spiritual witnesses the fleshly acts of someone who walks according to the flesh, he then may attempt to restore the fallen one. This verse does not say, "If one who is spiritual hears about someone being overtaken in a fault, he is to restore him." It does not say, "If one who is spiritual suspicions that a brother has been overtaken in a fault, he is to restore him." It is very plain that before the guilt is assumed, it must be proved. Before one is assumed guilty, he must be "overtaken" in a fault.

2. *The word, "fault," would include any of the works of the flesh mentioned in Galatians 5:19-21.*

3. *The word, "spiritual," is one who embraces all of Galatians 5:22 and 23.*

4. *The word, "restore," means "to give back."* It is the same word used concerning Zacchaeus, who, when he was converted, restored fourfold to all of those against whom he had sinned. The word means to bring one back where he was. This does not mean that a person who is fallen is still qualified to do everything that he used to do without a time of proving and testing. It DOES mean, however, that the one who is fallen should be brought back where he was as far as his relationship with the brethren are concerned. He should be accepted with the same open arms as before, with the same love as before, with the same compassion as before, with the same tenderness as before, with the same grace as before, with the same mercy as before and with the same fellowship as before.

5. *The word, "meekness," is a very interesting word.* It implies an evenness. It is often used concerning objects which are the same all the way through, such as homogenized milk in contrast to milk where the cream rises to the top. When the Lord Jesus said, "Blessed are the meek," He was saying in a sense, "Blessed are the equal ones," or "Blessed are the ones who look up to no one and down to no one," but "Blessed are the ones who look with a level eye to everyone." "Blessed are the ones who think themselves no worse than anyone and no better than anyone."

The story is told about a Baptist church in Washington, D.C. Many years ago Chief Justice Charles Evans Hughes, it is said, joined this particular Baptist church. Many others joined this particular Baptist church that same morning. As the names were read, Chief Justice Hughes was on one end of the line and a poor young man from a minority race was on the other end of the line. Of course, the pastor started off with the name of Chief Justice Hughes, when immediately Mr. Hughes interrupted the pastor and said, "Pastor, start at the other end of the line. The ground is level at the foot of the cross!" This is what our Lord is saying in Galatians 6:1. He is reminding us that we are to look down on no one, and even as we restore a fallen one, we are not to feel or act in a superior way. We are no better than he.

Neath the light of a kerosene lamp, beside the heat of a wood stove, with windows stuffed with newspapers to stop the howling wind from entering, with an outhouse in the backyard and a well off the back porch, my little mother used to point to me with a poverty-stricken finger and say, "Son, you are better than nobody, and you are as good as anybody! Look down to none; look up to none! Look everybody square in the eye! We don't wear the clothes that others wear, and we can't afford the house that others can afford, and we can't drive a car like others drive, but you are as good as anybody. But son, never let the day come when you feel that you are better than anybody!" This is what God is telling us here. The restorer is not to look down on the restored.

6. *The word, "considering," means "watching."* This means

watching yourself, not watching the restored one! We must realize the possibility of the restorer entering into the same sin that was committed by the restored, and one of the easiest ways to commit such a sin is to keep our eyes on the sinner rather than on the Saviour, and to be watching the life of the restored one rather than our own.

We are reminded by the Apostle that all of us are capable of committing the sins of the rest of us, and that there is no temptation given to one of us that is not given to all of us. **I Corinthians 10:13, "There hath no temptation taken you but such as is common to man: but God is faithful, Who will not suffer you to be tempted above that ye are able; but will with the temptation also make a way to escape, that ye may be able to bear it."** God is telling us in Galatians 6:1 that one of the main reasons we are to look everybody square in the eye as equals and look down on none is that if we do feel superior to the restored, we may ourselves be tempted by the same temptation he faced and enter into the same sin that he committed.

7. *The words, "also be tempted," are noteworthy.* This takes us back to Galatians 5:19-21. God is telling us here that those of us who live in the Spirit as in Galatians 5:22 and 23 possess the potential of committing any or all of the works of the flesh in Galatians 5:19-21.

8. *The word, "bear," in Galatians 6:2 implies that we are to bear the guilt of the fallen and restored one.* Then the word "burdens" in Galatians 6:2 teaches us that we are to enter into the yoke with them and to pull with them in order to help them to win the victory and gain strength. God is telling us here that when one sins, all have sinned. It would be a wonderful day for churches when every member takes the blame for the sin of one and realizes that the sin of one is really the sin of all.

When Achan took the forbidden gold, silver and garment from Jericho, God said, "Israel hath sinned." Oh, yes, Achan actually committed the sin, but all of Israel had a part in it. It will be a wonderful day in our churches when, if a young person goes into sin, the Pastor will say, "I have sinned." The Sunday school teacher will say, "I have sinned." The departmental superintendent will say, "I have sinned." The youth director will say, "I have sinned." The director of the youth choir will say, "I have sinned." The teacher in the Christian school will say, "I have sinned." The coach will say, "I have sinned." The parents will say, "I have sinned." The teaching is very plain. An individual's sin is a corporate sin, for had we not failed in some way, the fallen would not have failed. Since we all have sinned when one has fallen, then we all should bear his burden, as in Galatians 6:2, "Bear ye one another's burdens, and so fulfil the law of Christ." We all should lift him up. We all should accept him back. We all should love him. Since the sin was a corporate one, then the work of restoration should be a corporate one, and the grace of restoration should be a corporate grace.

9. *The words in Galatians 6:2, "fulfil the law of Christ," can be accomplished and completed only when we have restored the fallen, have realized that we too have fallen in him, and we all have joined in the act of restoration and in the grace of forgiveness.*

Now what is this law of Christ? I think it deals with **I John 2:1, "My little children, these things write I unto you, that ye sin not. And if any man sin, we have an advocate with the Father, Jesus Christ the righteous."** What a beautiful passage! It is addressed to little children, perhaps babes in Christ, those to whom it would be easy to fall. The first admonition is that they sin not. God hates sin, and God does not want us to sin.

Then He immediately tells us what His law of behavior is when we do sin. He does not say, "If any man sin, he loses his salvation." He does not say, "If any man sin, he is the object of God's disgust." He says, "If any man sin, we have an advocate with the Father." Notice the first person plural, "we." The Apostle was including himself as a sinner and as potentially in need of the reclamation mentioned in the following words of the verse.

Now notice the word, "advocate." This is the word, "paraclete," which is translated "comforter" elsewhere in the Scripture. It means "someone to run to another's side." God is saying here that

He does not want us to sin, but that if we do sin, we have someone to run to our side, and who is that someone? Praise the Lord, it is Jesus Christ the righteous! When a Christian falls, Jesus runs to his side to pick him up.

When I was a little boy, nearly all the streets we lived on were dirt or gravel roads. I would often run to Mother and ask if I could go across the street and play with a friend. She would say, "Why, of course, son, but be careful crossing the street. Stop before you cross, look both ways, and don't run! You may fall on the gravel." I assured her that I would obey, but as I got closer to the street, my little boyfriend would scream and say, "Hurry up, Jack! Hurry!" so I would run across the street, lose my footing in the gravel, fall, and skin my little knee. My mother would immediately come running to my side. She was disappointed in me, but she did not spank me. She took me back into the house, wiped off my knee and cleaned me up, put some medicine on the knee and perhaps a bandage. I said, "Mommy, can I still go across the street and play?"

She said, "Yes, you may, but son, I am telling you again: Don't disobey Mother and run. If you do disobey Mother, I'm going to have to bring you in the house and make you sit beside me while I iron so I can keep my eyes on you." I would go to the yard and start for the street. Then I would get excited again and rush across the street, only to fall the second time. Mother would rush to my side the second time and repeat the care. She would lift me up, take me into the house, wash me off, care for whatever scratch or cut I may have and then she would say, "Son, now if you run across that street this time, I'm not going to let you go across the street to play. You will have to come in and sit beside me while I iron so I can keep my eyes on you." I promised that I would walk across the street, but I forgot the promise, and in the excitement of getting to my little friend, I stumbled and fell again. Mother ran to my side, picked me up and very kindly took me into the house and sat me on a chair beside the ironing board so she could keep her eyes on me.

This is exactly what our blessed Saviour does. When we fall, He runs to our side to pick us up. He takes care of our wounds and reminds us not to sin again. When we sin again, He runs to our side to pick us up and takes care of our wounds and once again reminds us not to sin. When we keep on sinning, He finally says, "Okay, I can't let you stay down there any more. I must bring you up to Heaven so I can keep My eyes on you." This He does. He is taking us to Heaven, which is basically called "the sin unto death," and is not an act of wrath or violence; it is another act of love. He does not want us to continue in sin, so in His mercy He brings us to Heaven so we can be with Him, and He can keep His eye on us.

This is what I think God means when He tells us to bear one another's burdens and so fulfil the law of Christ. When a brother falls, we are to join Jesus in running to him. In fact, in some cases, we are to be Jesus running to him, for as much as we have done it unto one of the least of these His brethren, we have done it unto Him.

Far too many of us would translate this Scripture in Galatians 6:1, "If a brother be overtaken in a fault, criticize him," or "If a brother be overtaken in a fault, slander him," or "If a brother be overtaken in a fault, try to ruin him," or "If a brother be overtaken in a fault, try to destroy him." In far too many cases, this is our manner of treatment to the fallen. Thank God, it is not His manner and it is not His desire for us to treat them in such a way.

**Mark 16:7, "But go your way, tell His disciples and Peter that He goeth before you into Galilee: there shall ye see Him, as He said unto you."** Notice the two words, "and Peter." What a blessed statement! The ladies have come to the tomb. They find the stone rolled away and a man dressed in white at the sepulchre. He is a messenger from God, and what is that message? "Go tell the disciples and Peter that Jesus is risen." Why did he single out Peter? We know why. At our Lord's crucifixion, Peter had joined himself with the wrong crowd. He had warmed himself by the Devil's fire, had walked afar off, and had denied the faith, the church and his Lord. He had even cursed. He was a fallen saint, not fallen from grace, but fallen in grace. Nevertheless, he was fallen. How sweet it is and how tender it is that God's messenger brought God's message that the ladies go and announce the resurrection of Christ to the disciples "and Peter." God was reminding us that He has a special love for the fallen. God loves all of us, but He has a special unique love for some. He says, "Go tell the disciples and the burdened," "Go tell the disciples and the lonely," "Go tell the disciples and the fallen."

I do not know all that is behind these two little words, "and Peter." Perhaps if he had not said "and Peter," they would not have told Peter, because perhaps they would not have thought of him as still being a disciple, or maybe God wanted Peter to know in a special way that He still loved him and that Peter still belonged to Him.

These two little words not only show His love for the fallen, but they show His care for the fallen and for each individual. God is saying, "Peter, the Christians may not care any more, but I do!" "The Christians may not be concerned about your restoration, but I am." "The Christians may have given up on you, but I haven't." So He gives the message to the angel to give: "Tell His disciples and Peter."

There is something else that God is saying with these two precious words, "and Peter." He is letting Peter know of His forgiveness. Can you imagine Peter getting the message that God had sent to him a special word? God was saying to Peter, "You are forgiven. I want you where you were. I love you as I loved you before. I need you as I needed you before. I care as much as I ever cared, and Peter, you are forgiven!"

At this moment this author is that messenger. He says to that person who has fallen whose eyes are scanning these pages: God said, "Go tell the disciples and you." And he says to the members of the church who have not fallen, "When you tell the good news, tell the fallen too. Include the fallen!"

Then God is also reminding us of His awareness. He was saying to Peter, "I know you are there. You may think you have gone so far that I cannot see you, but you haven't! I know your address! I know where you live! I know where you work! I know your motives! I am aware of you, Peter, and you won't get beyond that awareness!"

How beautiful! How wonderfully sweet that God sent His messenger to tell of His resurrection, and to send the ladies to tell the disciples . . . and Peter!

May God help His churches to love the fallen, to pray for the fallen, to run to the fallen, to lift up the fallen, to welcome the fallen, to strengthen the fallen, to carry the burden of the fallen, to share the guilt of the fallen and, by God's grace, to reclaim and restore the fallen!

# Chapter 3

# Treatment of the Weak

**Romans 14:1, "Him that is weak in the faith receive ye, but not to doubtful disputations."**

The word, "weak," in this passage means "without power" or "little power."

I have often said that there are four groups of people in the First Baptist Church of Hammond. Group #1 is composed of those who accept what the preacher says because the preacher says it. Group #2 is composed of those who believe what the preacher says and accept it because they already believed it. Somewhere else they were grounded in the faith, and then to their surprise they found someone who agreed with them years after they thought such preachers were extinct. Group #3 is that group of people who listen to what the preacher says, consider the pros and cons and decide whether or not to accept it. Group #4 is that group of people in the church who believe nothing the preacher says, but they love to hear him say it. Now it matters not whether these four groups comprise the membership of a local church, but one thing is for sure: There are different degrees of strength among our church members! Some church members are strong. Some have fallen, some are heartbroken, and, yes, some are weak. The Bible does not leave us in wonder about the treatment of these weak ones.

Notice again **Romans 14:1, "Him that is weak in the faith receive ye, but not to doubtful disputations."** Notice especially the words, "in the faith." These are saved people about whom the Apostle is speaking. Yet, they are weak Christians.

1. *We are to receive them.* Notice the words, "receive ye." God is telling us to receive the weak in the faith. This means that we are to welcome them. We are to have special interest in them. We are not to remind them of their weakness, but we are to accept them as brothers in Christ and make them feel as one of us, for, of a fact, they are.

2. *We are not to receive them to "doubtful disputations."* We are not to engage in arguments with them about our differences. This is what preaching is for! This is what Bible teaching is for!

This is explained in **Romans 14:2 and 3, "For one believeth that he may eat all things: another, who is weak, eateth herbs. Let not him that eateth despise him that eateth not; and let not him which eateth not judge him that eateth: for God hath received him."** Here we have one Christian who eats meats and another who is a vegetarian. They are not to engage in doubtful disputations.

We find another example in **verses 5 and 6, "One man esteemeth one day above another: another esteemeth every day alike. Let every man be fully persuaded in his own mind. He that regardeth the day, regardeth it unto the Lord; and he that regardeth not the day, to the Lord he doth not regard it. He that eateth, eateth to the Lord, for he giveth God thanks: and he that eateth not, to the Lord he eateth not, and giveth God thanks."** One Christian observes a certain day; another Christian does not. They are not to engage in doubtful disputations concerning this. One Christian observes Easter as a holy day. Another strong Christian who knows the Bible knows that Easter is not a holy day. **Colossians 2:14-17, "Blotting out the handwriting of ordinances that was against us, which was contrary to us, and took it out of the way, nailing it to His cross; and having spoiled principalities and powers, He made a shew of them openly, triumphing over them in it. Let no man therefore judge you in meat, or in drink, or in respect of an holyday, or of the new**

**moon, or of the sabbath days: which are a shadow of things to come; but the body is of Christ."** God is telling us that we should not get with the weaker brother and argue with him about such matters.

I preach all over America. Nearly every week I am with someone who would disagree with me on some matter that could be called a doubtful disputation. For example, I do not believe a church choir should wear robes. I go to many churches whose choirs are robed. I do not engage in doubtful disputations with the pastor concerning this matter.

I go to churches whose music is different from ours. It is not sinful music; it is just not what we prefer here at First Baptist Church. I do not engage in doubtful disputations concerning this matter.

3. *We are to withdraw ourselves from every weak brother who has a disorderly walk.* **II Thessalonians 3:6, "Now we command you, brethren, in the name of our Lord Jesus Christ, that ye withdraw yourselves from every brother that walketh disorderly, and not after the tradition which he received of us."** This does not mean that we are to be unkind to anyone. The Bible is very plain concerning our grace and kindness to all, but it is also very plain concerning the fact that we are not to engage in social life or in regular fellowship with some Christians. I do not believe for a second that this is talking about church membership. I do not believe it is talking about the weak person or the disorderly person not being welcome in the church services. I think God is telling the individual Christians to watch the crowd with whom they run and to associate with strong Christians. The word "withdraw" means to "bend away." Though we are to be nice to people who walk disorderly, we are certainly not supposed to run with their crowd.

The word "disorderly" here is a military term which means "out of step" or "out of rank." Of course, in the light of all Scripture we are to be gracious and kind, forbearing and patient with these weak ones, but we should not walk with them, spend long seasons of time with them, unless, of course, we are helping them to become stronger by teaching them the Word or explaining to them the Christian life.

This is explained again in **II Thessalonians 3:14, "And if any man obey not our word by this epistle, note that man, and have no company with him, that he may be ashamed."** Note the words, "have no company with him." This means we are not to mingle with them. Sure, we see them at church. We shake their hands. We welcome them. We try to strengthen them, but we do not enter into social activities with them. Often Christians attempt to do so in order to strengthen the weak, and inevitably such a relationship weakens the strong!

We have the same teaching in **I Corinthians 5:11, "But now I have written unto you not to keep company, if any man that is called a brother be a fornicator, or covetous, or an idolater, or a railer, or a drunkard, or an extortioner; with such an one no not to eat."** Notice especially the words, "not to keep company." Once again we have the idea of not mixing, mingling, or socializing with them.

Some of the sins of these weak ones are mentioned in verse 11. Of course, we all know what a fornicator is. We all know what an idolater is. We know what a drunkard is. We know what an extortioner is. The word "covetous" means "greedy." The word "railer" means "an evil speaker" or "critical." It is very plain that with people who criticize, people who are greedy, people who are fornicators, people who are drunkards, people who are extortioners, etc., we are not to keep company!

Notice the last eight words of **I Corinthians 5:11, "with such an one no not to eat."** Here we have a simple explanation. Eating is a sign of socializing, a symbol of sharing pleasures and fellowship. This means that if someone is critical and asks you to go out to eat with him, you are not supposed to go. You are supposed to be nice to him and courteous to him and kind to him, but you are not supposed to have time to accept his invitation and go out to eat. What God is saying is that He does not want us to sit down and socialize with the weak Christian, whether he be greedy, a fornicator or a critic. Now, of course, in our Christian society the fornicator is in a class far beneath the critic, but in God's economy they are in the same class, and though we are to be kind and gracious to both, we are not to keep company, mix, mingle, socialize or sit down to eat with them.

About the same thing is mentioned in **Psalm 1:1-3, "Blessed is the man that walketh not in the counsel of the ungodly, nor standeth in the way of sinners, nor sitteth in the seat of the scornful. But his delight is in the law of the Lord; and in His law doth he meditate day and night. And he shall be like a tree planted by the rivers of water, that bringeth forth his fruit in his season; his leaf also shall not wither; and whatsoever he doeth shall prosper."** Notice that we are not to walk in the counsel of the ungodly. We are not to stand in the way of sinners. We are not to sit in the seat of the scornful. In other words, we are not to run or walk with the weak Christian (that is, the fornicator, greedy, idolater, drunkard, gossip or critic). We are not to stand around with him. We are not to sit down to converse with him unless we are teaching him spiritual things.

4. *We are to support the weak.* **I Thessalonians 5:14, "Now we exhort you, brethren, warn them that are unruly, comfort the feebleminded, support the weak, be patient toward all men." Acts 20:35, "I have shewed you all things, how that so labouring ye ought to support the weak, and to remember the words of the Lord Jesus, how He said, It is more blessed to give than to receive."** This verse implies that we are to be like an anchor. We stay the same. We are not supposed to be pulled away from our position by them! This, in many cases, will happen if we socialize with them, but we are to be the anchor, the unswerving, unwavering, unchanging rock to which they can hold. We don't sip cocktails with them so we can help them! We don't go mixed bathing with them so we can let them know we are "good old boys." We don't use their language in order to attempt to straighten them. We stay solid. We believe what we always believed. We stand where we always stood. They can lean on us for support.

This does not mean that we are to support their weakness; it means we are to support the weak by our being strong and unwavering. The word, "support," here is used concerning a foundation. We are to be the foundation on which the weak can stand, the rock on which they can lean, and when they decide to come back, they will find us where they left us, living in the same Book, walking with the same God, standing on the same truths, living with the same convictions. If they come back and find us gone, we cannot support them.

5. *We are to bear the infirmities of the weak.* **Romans 15:1, "We then that are strong ought to bear the infirmities of the weak, and not to please ourselves."** This means patience toward their weakness, but not acceptance of it. This means that we should be longsuffering with them while they are in sin, but in no way leave the impression that we condone the sin.

In summary, the Christian is to receive the weak, support the weak, love the weak, be kind to the weak, help strengthen the weak and do all within his power to lead him back to Christian strength. On the other hand, he is not to socialize with him or mix and mingle with him in a social manner.

As a young preacher in east Texas many years ago I got to thinking one day, and I realized that I was chasing off the people who were not full- grown. I expected everyone to carry the load that I carried. I was not willing to get anything from those from whom I could not get everything. I was destroying the people who did not give all. It was sort of an "all or nothing at all" situation. I distinctly remember the day when I decided to accept Christians as they are and do my best to make them what they ought to be.

At that time I sought some answers concerning my weak people, and I came up with several reasons why they were weak, as follows:

1. *Some were carrying too light a load.* They could not become strong because they did not carry a heavy enough load to make them strong. I read **Galatians 6:1-6, "Brethren, if a man be overtaken in a fault, ye which are spiritual, restore such an one in the spirit of meekness; considering thyself, lest thou also be**

tempted. **Bear ye one another's burdens, and so fulfil the law of Christ. For if a man think himself to be something, when he is nothing, he deceiveth himself. But let every man prove his own work, and then shall he have rejoicing in himself alone, and not in another. For every man shall bear his own burden. Let him that is taught in the word communicate unto him that teacheth in all good things."** I then read **Matthew 11:28, 29, "Come unto Me, all ye that labour and are heavy laden, and I will give you rest. Take My yoke upon you, and learn of Me; for I am meek and lowly in heart: and ye shall find rest unto your souls."**

Recently I was talking to a young man. He shared the burden of his heart with me, and believe me, he did have a heavy burden! After we had talked for awhile, I suggested that we pray together. He prayed first. He started off by praying, "Dear Lord, take away my burden." Before I knew it, I had interrupted his prayer, and I said, "Lord, don't do it." (This is so unlike me. I do not ever recall doing such a thing before.) He looked up and said, "Brother Hyles, don't you think God ought to take my burden away?"

I said, "No, I don't."

He then bowed his head and began to pray again. He prayed, "Lord, then don't take my burden away. Give me strength to bear my burden."

To my surprise I interrupted again and said, "Lord, don't do it!"

He stopped praying again and asked me why I had asked the Lord not to give him strength to bear his burden.

I told him, "Son, you don't get strength for your burdens; you get strength from your burdens. The burden is what makes you strong. The strongest Christians are those who have the most burdens, and they did not get strong in order to bear their burdens; they got strong by bearing their burdens."

Suppose a young man asked his parents for a set of weights for Christmas. Sure enough, he receives them as a gift from his parents. The young man doesn't look at the weights and say, "Lord, take my burden away." No, he asked for the burden; he requested it because he wanted to be strong. Neither did the young man say, "Lord, make me strong enough to lift these weights." Not at all! The very purpose of the weights was to make him strong. If he were strong enough to lift the weights before he got them, he didn't need them.

It seems that almost every time a Christian has problems, he attributes it to the Devil. Preachers say to me often, "The Devil sure is fighting." Now it just may be that God is giving you a set of weights for Christmas in order to make you strong.

In cities all over America football players are in weight rooms. They are not enjoying the perspiring, the groaning, the grunting that they are doing, but they want to be strong. They have a battle to fight on football fields across America. If they win the battle, they must be strong. If they are strong, they must have burdens to bear and weights to lift.

There are battles that the Christian must fight. In order to win, he must be strong. If he is strong, he has to lift some weights; he has to pump some iron; he has to have some burdens. The more the weights and the bigger the weights, the stronger is the man. The more the burdens and the bigger the burdens that the Christian bears, the stronger he becomes, but many of our people are weak because they bear too light a load.

2. *Many are weak because they bear too soon a load.* A few days after someone is converted, we approach him about teaching a Sunday school class, and before long he is so burdened down that the load is too heavy for him to bear. Bear in mind, the weight lifter starts off with the light weights first and gradually increases the load that he lifts.

3. *Some are weak because they carry too heavy a load.* A novice weight lifter does not start by bench pressing 300 pounds. That is too heavy a load for him. Many Christians have taken up a load that was too heavy instead of gradually coming to that load, and they have been unable to lift the weights. A young man who is given a set of weights cannot get strong by trying to pick up a weight that he cannot lift. It is the lifting of the weight that makes one strong, and the weight lifted must be one that can be lifted! No one gets strong pulling on a weight that remains on the floor. Care must be taken

not to overload the Christian and give him too heavy a load. This will cause him to be weak.

4. *Many are weak because they have the wrong kind of load.* Each Christian should know what type of a load he can carry. For example, I have many assistant pastors. Their load levels are different. Their talents and gifts are different. I must be careful not to place them in areas where they are not capable. Many Christians have been given tasks for which they were not suited. They became discouraged and later, weak.

"Weak" is a relative term. There are degrees of weakness and degrees of strength. It is easy for someone who is strong to become impatient with one who is weak. It is also easy for the strong ones to become critical of the weak and even to disdain them. Some in our churches look at the weak with disgust. On the other hand, others choose the weak as fellow-socializers and best friends. Neither of these positions is the wise one. The wise and Scriptural position is for the strong Christian to encourage, to support, to receive and to be kind to the weak. On the other hand, he is not to expose himself to unnecessary interaction with him, lest the weakness become contagious and the strong becomes weak instead of the weak becoming strong.

Now read **Romans 16:17, "Now I beseech you, brethren, mark them which cause divisions and offences contrary to the doctrine which ye have learned; and avoid them."** The word, "avoid" here does not mean "to shun." It does not condone the action of the Pharisee. It simply means to "bend away" from them.

There is no doctrine in the Bible any more plainly presented than the doctrine of separation, and the Word of God is filled with examples of people who did not practice this separation. Consequently, they were led to ruin. Balaam sold a nation into intermarriage with idolaters because he ran with the wrong crowd. Jehoshaphat destroyed his nation by running with the wrong crowd and associating with the wicked King Ahab and his rebellious wife, Jezebel. This association led Jehoshaphat's son to marry Athaliah, the daughter of Ahab and Jezebel. What Jezebel did to the northern kingdom, Athaliah did to the southern kingdom. Before Peter cursed, swore and denied the faith, he was warming at the wrong fire and following the Lord afar off with the wrong crowd. Choosing to run with the wrong crowd ruined Lot, turned his wife to a pillar of salt, and wrecked the lives of his children and their children. Running with the wrong crowd caused Abraham to father a heathen nation begun by his illegitimate son, Ishmael.

The Bible is very plain. We are not to run with the wrong crowd. And, yes, there is a wrong crowd in every church and every Christian school! We are to love them, to support them, to receive them, to be kind to them, to be gracious to them, to be patient with them, but we are not to keep company with them, according to I Corinthians 5:11. When we embrace their weakness, we do not strengthen them; we meet them on their level instead of on ours. We strengthen them by holding our position and remaining strong so they will have an anchor that is firm and a foundation that is solid when they return. Hence, they become strong because of our strength. This is God's plan concerning our treatment of the weak.

# Chapter 4

# Treatment of the Strong

In every area of our lives we need strength around us. One of the weaknesses of our society is the attempt by the masses to weaken the strong. Business needs strong management and labor will be wise to keep it so. Many a business has gone under because labor weakened management, thereby killing the goose that laid the golden egg.

The same thing is true concerning politics. We need a strong President, and the opposing political party is very unwise in its attempt to weaken the power of the presidency and of the President. He needs our support, our prayers and our encouragement for him to be strong.

One of the sad things about the press in our nation is its constant attempt to weaken leadership with its constant desire to sell papers and magazines. It continues to explore and seek the weaknesses of the strong in an effort for the spectacular to be printed. In so doing, we are lessening our own security by weakening the ones who offer it to us.

In professional sports we are seeing the same thing. The athlete gets rich at the expense of the owners, not realizing that to weaken the ownership may someday cost him his job and destroy the sport by which he makes his livelihood.

America needs strength! Wise is that nation that strengthens the hands of its leadership, which in turn can offer security and protection to followship.

Thank God for strong people! However, even in our churches they often tend to be disliked. We love to pull for the underdog, and there is something in us that wants to see the strong toppled, but we need the strong, and when they fall they fall on us and rob us of a security that we need from strength.

Our nation is in desperate need of some heroes. Baseball needs a Babe Ruth, a Dizzy Dean, a Ted Williams and a Joe DiMaggio. Football needs a Red Grange and Bronko Nagurski. Boxing needs a Jack Dempsey and a Joe Louis. Golf needs an Arnold Palmer, a Ben Hogan and a Bob Jones. Politics needs a Theodore Roosevelt and a George Washington. The military needs a Douglas Mac-Arthur, a General George Patton. The pulpit needs a Dwight Moody, a Billy Sunday and a Charles Spurgeon. Law enforcement needs a J. Edgar Hoover. Coaching needs a Vince Lombardi or a George Halas. This is not the day for the hero or the legend. We seem to want to pull them down to our level. We want to homogenize everybody, and we even attack the principles of the dead in order to destroy yesterday's heroes while we destroy today's. We flounder for lack of leadership and at the same time attempt to make leadership flounder.

We should encourage strong people. They are the most lonely people in the church. They are the most criticized people in the church, and they need our love, respect and confidence in order to compensate for those who are trying to shoot them down.

In doing this we must be careful to understand that strength has weakness, and we must not be disenchanted with our heroes when we discover that they too are made of flesh.

I have known personally and intimately the greatest preachers of this and the last generation. I was a warm personal friend to Dr. Bob Jones, Sr. I knew in a very personal way Dr. R. G. Lee and was an honorary pallbearer at his funeral. For 22 years I traveled with Dr. John R. Rice, and perhaps I knew him better than anybody on earth except for his own family. I preached his funeral message. I was a close friend of Dr. Bill Rice, and for over a third of a century I was a good friend with Evangelist Lester Roloff. I spoke at the funeral service for Dr. Bill Rice and also preached Dr. Roloff's funeral message. Dr. Ford Porter was my good friend, and I preached his funeral message. Then, of course, I shared the same platform with such men as Jacob Gartenhaus, B. R. Lakin, G. B. Vick and others. They were all great men, and they were all my heroes, but I was well aware that each was human and possessed weaknesses. Some of them fought each other, thereby revealing to me their humanity, but in no way taking from me my estimation of their greatness.

We must thank God for the strong. We must realize their humanity, but we must not let that realization shake our confidence in them. They are great men, not perfect men. They are strong men, but not omnipotent men. They are wise men, but not omniscient men. We need men of their caliber as our leaders.

Paul was a great man and Peter was a great man; yet they had personal problems between themselves. **Galatians 2:11, "But when Peter was come to Antioch, I withstood him to the face, because he was to be blamed."**

Barnabas was a great man and Paul was a great man, but they were human as is manifested in **Acts 15:36-40, "And some days after Paul said unto Barnabas, Let us go again and visit our brethren in every city where we have preached the Word of the Lord, and see how they do. And Barnabas determined to take with them John, whose surname was Mark. But Paul thought not good to take him with them, who departed from them from Pamphylia, and went not with them to the work. And the contention was so sharp between them, that they departed asunder one from the other: and so Barnabas took Mark, and sailed unto Cyprus; and Paul chose Silas, and departed, being recommended by the brethren unto the grace of God."** They had a sharp disagreement.

John Wesley and George Whitefield had problems getting along together. The same is true with Calvin and Luther, Harry Truman and Douglas MacArthur and many other great men. Though we should not deify them and should accept them as human, we still need to exalt them, to pray for them, to honor them and to strengthen them in order that they in turn as our leaders may give us strength and direction.

In every church there are strong men—men with leadership ability—men whom the church needs. Such men should be respected, prayed for, honored and followed. They should not be open game for criticism and gossip! Because of their strength they may not be as likable as others in the church. Because of their strong wills, their manner may not be as palatable as that of more gentle people, but we need them and should hold them up before the Lord and encourage them.

Every church has some ladies who are more zealous than others. Their manner may not be as gentle and as appealing because they are leaders of the ladies and girls. They are needed. Such ladies lead departments in the Sunday school, direct children's choirs, build ladies' Sunday school classes, work as supervisors in college dormitories, teach in the Christian school and perform multitudes of other important tasks in the work of God. Because of their leadership abilities as they lead other women and children, they are often the object of criticism, especially by men, and especially by men who are not strong leaders and have become jealous of the leadership ability of the ladies who are leaders. Don't misunderstand me; I am not advocating that ladies lead men. The Bible is very plain about that, but let us thank God for those ladies who are strong and who can administrate in areas where men would not and could not lead. May God's people look at the strong and thank God for them.

We are all flesh, and the best of us is weak, but God has ordained that every human organization have leadership. A city needs a mayor. A state needs a governor. A nation needs a king or a president or a prime minister. A team needs a coach. A school needs a principal. A church needs a pastor. A business needs an executive. A college needs a president. A classroom needs a teacher. A dormitory needs a supervisor. Now we must choose the strong from among us to fill these positions. When chosen they should be admired, loved and honored. When the team weakens the coach, games are lost. When the student weakens the teacher, he weakens his education. When the country weakens the president, it weakens its national security. When a church weakens a pastor, it loses its power. When a state or a city weakens its governor or mayor, it promotes anarchy and confusion.

Let us not fall for Satan's method of luring the follower into criticism and jealousy of the leader. We do not strengthen ourselves when we weaken the strong; we rather weaken ourselves when we weaken the strong, for God has given us the strong to strengthen us. Anarchy not only weakens the nation, but it weakens the people of that nation, and those who are guilty of anarchy are weaker than they would have been had they been submissive. A submissive people is a strong people. A submissive team is a strong team. A submissive student body forms a good school. A submissive membership makes a great church. Any other plan is one that is derived from Satan himself when, as an archangel, he rebelled against God and sought to exalt himself above God and set himself on God's throne. In so doing, he hurt himself! He certainly did not hurt God! God was still God after Satan's rebellion, but Satan was no longer an archangel, and his angels were no longer God's angels. He and his angels fell! Followers always fall when they topple their leaders!

At this point in American history a tragic thing is happening. Liberal politicians seem to have more animosity toward Mr. Reagan than they do toward Mr. Gorbachev. They spend more time attacking American conservatism than they do attacking Russian communism, and an excessive hatred of communism seems to be a greater crime than communism itself. The liberal politicians seem bent on joining the liberal press for the destruction of any conservative leader who is strong. Then that conservative leader represents our nation at summit meetings. His hands are tied. His power is limited. His plans are paralyzed, and the weak leader that we have created goes to represent us. By the time he is at the treaty table, he has been made so powerless by his own fellow-Americans that his position is weakened—not because of the attack of the enemy but because of the attack from our own citizens!

The same is true in a church. Parents often feel that there is some merit in criticizing the pastor. Perhaps it gives them some sense of power if they can speak ill of a strong leader. Their children hear this ill-speaking and lose confidence in the pastor. Then the day comes when the child needs the pastor and only the pastor can help, but by that time the child has lost confidence in his preacher! The parents have weakened the leader so that the leader cannot help their own flesh and blood.

Not only are we trying to weaken leadership and in so doing weaken ourselves, but we are trying to destroy people who have been gone from the scene for years. Not only do we want to tear down today's heroes; we want to destroy yesterday's heroes. Not only does the liberal press, the liberal politician and the liberal educator seek to homogenize all of us today and seek to bring down any strong leader, but they unite in attacking the memory of our past heroes, so they investigate in order to find everything negative possible about J. Edgar Hoover, George Washington, Douglas MacArthur, Dwight Eisenhower, Babe Ruth and others.

America's youth today are looking for heroes. Let us help them find some. Let us close ranks and thank God for those who are strong and pray for God to give us other strong people whom we may follow, encourage and strengthen!

Someone has said that preaching is pouring back to the congregation in a flood what is received from them in a vapor. Some few, thank God, can capture this vapor, translate it into a flood and return it to the audience. Leadership is the same way. Let us constantly send them the vapor so that they may return to us a flood!

# Chapter 5

# Treatment of the Heartbroken

Ezekiel 34:3, "Ye eat the fat, and ye clothe you with the wool, ye kill them that are fed: but ye feed not the flock."

Isaiah 61:1, "The Spirit of the Lord God is upon me; because the Lord hath anointed me to preach good tidings unto the meek; he hath sent me to bind up the brokenhearted, to proclaim liberty to the captives, and the opening of the prison to them that are bound."

One of the main purposes of a church is its ministry to the heartbroken. Someone has said, "He who preaches to broken hearts will never want for a congregation." I have often said that behind every face there is a broken heart, and behind every smile there is a reason to cry. As I look out over my congregation on a Sunday morning, I see those whose hearts are broken because of incurable illnesses in their own body or in the body of a loved one. I see those whose hearts are broken because they are under attack; they are suffering severe criticism or are objects of a malicious scandal. I see a couple whose daughter has just left her husband to run off with another man. I see a lady whose daughter is pregnant and not married. I see a lady whose husband has just left her to rear the children alone. I see a man whose business has just faced bankruptcy. I see a family whose son has broken their hearts. I see children whose daddy has just forsaken them, and I see multitudes of others whose hearts are broken. God's people should take extra care in their treatment of these brokenhearted saints.

1. *Act as near normal as possible.* They want to know of your love, but they don't want to be singled out for special attention. Just let them know that nothing has changed. Assure them that your relationship is the same as always, but do not do this verbally. Do it by treating them as you always have. Just let them know by your normal treatment that all is the same.

2. *It is usually best not to mention their problem.* To do so may open a wound that has been closing. It may cause a fresh hurt that is unnecessary. It is often best not to say such things as, "I heard about your burden," "I know about your problem," etc.

3. *Do not try to figure out why.* It is so easy for God's people to become an Eliphaz, a Zophar or a Bildad, who were the "friends" of Job. One of them came and said, "Job, I know why you are having your trouble; you are not spiritual enough!" Another came and said, "Job, I know why you are having your trouble; you have left the traditions of the fathers!" Another came and said, "Job, I know why are having your trouble; you have sinned and are being punished!" The truth is that none of us knows why God does what He does, and more often than not, God's people face troubles and heartache because of reasons other than punishment for sin. It is not our job to figure out why; it is our job to be loving, thoughtful and helpful when our brothers and sisters have broken hearts.

4. *Don't tell them of any criticism that you have heard.* Years ago we had a man in our church who walked with me from my office to the pulpit on a regular basis. Just before I would leave him to walk to the platform, he would put his arm around me or take my hand and with emotion say something like this: "I'm for you, Preacher . . . no matter what they say!" All during the service I kept wondering, "What did they say?" The truth is, that man loved me, but he did not comfort me.

One little girl wrote me a note and said, "Dear Brother Hyles. I love you in spite of the fact that nobody else does." Somehow or other that note was not as comforting to me as it was intended to be!

Recently a member of the church who is a very lovely Christian came to me and said, "Brother Hyles, I want you to know that my family is for you in this battle." Then I started to wonder, "What is the battle? What battle are they talking about?"

5. *Use unsaid words to express sympathy.* Perhaps a squeeze of the hand, a pat on the back, or a touch of the elbow is all that is necessary. With those little gestures one is saying, "Everything is the same. Nothing has changed. I still have confidence in you, and I still love you. I am still your friend, and I still think you are a good Christian."

6. *Show confidence in them.* Not long ago a preacher friend of mine had his heart broken by the actions of a married child. As soon as I heard of it, I talked with him and asked him if he would be a speaker on a program with me. This was simply an expression of my saying, "I still have confidence in you, and I'm your friend! Nothing has changed!"

Several years ago I had a man lined up to come to speak for one of the ministries of our church. Between the time that he was scheduled and the time for the speaking engagement, he had a broken heart that could have made him fearful that some of us had lost confidence in him. I did not write him and tell him what I had heard. I did not call him to assure him of my love in spite of his broken heart. I simply wrote him a little note confirming his speaking engagement with me and telling him that I was looking forward to having him. That was all that was necessary. His heart was broken. I did not want to remind him of the cause, but I simply wanted him to know that nothing had changed.

Express your love and friendship to the heartbroken. There are many ways that this could be done. Years ago when some slander had been spoken by wicked tongues concerning my good friend, Dr. John R. Rice, my heart was grieved! A few days later we were speaking together. As he walked on the platform and sat down beside me, I reached over and squeezed his knee and said simply, "I'm your friend." Years passed. Careless lips and malicious tongues chose to speak evil of me. The next time Dr. Rice and I were together, he reached over from his chair on the platform and squeezed my knee and whispered, "I'm your friend." He did not need to say any more. I knew what he meant. On one occasion Dr. Curtis Hutson did the same thing to me, and as I remember on another occasion, I did the same thing to him.

Many years ago Evangelist Charles Weigle suffered the heartbreak of his life. His wife decided she did not want to be a preacher's wife. She took their child and left him. The great heart of Dr. Lee Roberson simply contacted Dr. Weigle and asked if he would come and live at Tennessee Temple College and Highland Park Baptist Church. Dr. Weigle agreed to do so. Dr. Roberson was simply saying to Dr. Weigle and the whole world, "I have confidence in you still. I love you still. I'm your friend still, and nothing has changed."

This love and friendship could be expressed by a gift sent seemingly for no reason at all, or an attractive card or a tender embrace or the touch of the hand or an arm around the shoulder.

The one consoling the heartbroken should not do it too strongly. Just let the brokenhearted one know that all is the same; nothing has changed.

7. *Try to decide for what the heartbroken person is reaching.* Some people want and feel that they need different means of expression of confidence and love. If you know someone well enough to know that they need more than the aforementioned reminders, give it to them. If you feel someone reaching out for a certain kind of assurance, give it to them.

Leaders need this kind of assurance as well as followers. I am thinking now about one of the greatest preachers in America whose daughter broke his heart, and he has had to rear her son. I am thinking of another one of the greatest preachers in America who one day on a platform pointed to the balcony and said to me, "Those two little girls up there are my granddaughters." His son had divorced his wife; the lady in the balcony with the two children was his former daughter-in-law, and the children were his grandchildren.

One of the ten best-known preachers in America had a daughter who went into the world, broke his heart and defied everything that her daddy preached. It is said that Billy Sunday stood to speak in a great tabernacle. Just as he began to speak, someone handed him a newspaper that told of his son committing an awful sin, and perhaps had been arrested. Supposedly Billy Sunday grabbed his chest and shouted, "Preach Christ," and slumped to the floor.

One of the greatest preachers in America had a son who became a liberal and destroyed the work of his dad after his dad passed away.

Heartbreak comes to everybody, in every walk of life and on every scale of spiritual growth and progress. Let us treat the heartbroken with a tender, subtle awareness that nothing has changed.

Before concluding this chapter, I must speak a word to the heartbroken. When something happens in your life that causes you to wonder if you will still be respected and accepted, don't withdraw from us! We still love you! You belong to us! We still have confidence in you! Let us have a chance to assure you of our love and confidence! Don't leave us! Don't leave your church and go to another! Stay with those who love you! You need them, and they need you! You need their love! They need to love you! You need their expression of confidence, and they need to give it!

# Chapter 6

# Treatment of Followers

**Ephesians 6:5-9, "Servants, be obedient to them that are your masters according to the flesh, with fear and trembling, in singleness of your heart, as unto Christ; not with eyeservice, as menpleasers; but as the servants of Christ, doing the will of God from the heart; with good will doing service, as to the Lord, and not to men: knowing that whatsoever good thing any man doeth, the same shall he receive of the Lord, whether he be bond or free. And, ye masters, do the same things unto them, forbearing threatening: knowing that your Master also is in heaven; neither is there respect of persons with Him."**

**Ruth 2:4, "And, behold, Boaz came from Bethlehem, and said unto the reapers, The Lord be with you. And they answered him, The Lord bless thee."**

In the New Testament there are three titles given for the main position in a New Testament church. One is the title of pastor; another is the title of elder; another is the title of bishop. All three of these titles represent the same position.

**I Peter 5:1-4, "The elders which are among you I exhort, who am also an elder, and a witness of the sufferings of Christ, and also a partaker of the glory that shall be revealed: Feed the flock of God which is among you, taking the oversight thereof, not by constraint, but willingly; not for filthy lucre, but of a ready mind; neither as being lords over God's heritage, but**

**being ensamples to the flock. And when the chief Shepherd shall appear, ye shall receive a crown of glory that fadeth not away."**

You will notice in these verses, all three of these titles are mentioned. They all deal with the same office. Each of these titles represents a unique treatment that the leader is to give to his followers. For example, the title of elder represents experience and wisdom. The leader is to give to the follower access to his wisdom. This could come through preaching, teaching, counseling, etc.

Now consider the title of pastor. This is another word for shepherd. The leader of the church is to give his followers the protection that a shepherd gives to the sheep. He is to warn the followers of things that would harm them even as the shepherd did to the sheep, and he is to stand vigil over them to keep these things from doing them harm.

The third title is that of bishop. This word means overseer. This means the pastor is the overseer of the follower. For the good of the follower, the pastor is to oversee all of the work of the church and be sure that it is done properly and that the follower may have the kind of church that he needs in order that he may be all that God wants him to be.

Much is said about the way the follower should treat the leader, and this is right. Not enough is said concerning the way the leader should treat the follower. Oh, yes, the follower is taught to obey his spiritual leader. **Hebrews 13:7, "Remember them which have the rule over you, who have spoken unto you the word of God: whose faith follow, considering the end of their conversation."** He is likewise taught to submit himself to his spiritual leader. **Hebrews 13:17, "Obey them that have the rule over you, and submit yourselves: for they watch for your souls, as they that must give account, that they may do it with joy, and not with grief: for that is unprofitable for you."** These are words that include having faith in, yielding to, giving in, following, etc. There are other places in the Bible that remind us that God's people are to follow the pastors.

Then there are Scriptures that remind the pastors regarding their treatment of other pastors. The New Testament church had a multiplicity of pastors. Each church would have several pastors, just as is the case in the First Baptist Church of Hammond. There is a certain way that these pastors are to treat each other. **I Timothy 1:1, 2, "Paul, an apostle of Jesus Christ by the commandment of God our Saviour, and Lord Jesus Christ, which is our hope; unto Timothy, my own son in the faith: Grace, mercy, and peace, from God our Father and Jesus Christ our Lord."** I Timothy 5:17, **"Let the elders that rule well be counted worthy of double honour, especially they who labour in the word and doctrine."** Read these verses carefully. Paul is writing to one elder, or pastor, Timothy. He is telling him how to treat other elders or pastors. In I Timothy 5:19 he reminds him that he is not to believe an accusation without witnesses. He reminds him of the respect and honor that he is to give to other pastors. Many pastors preach and teach from these passages in an effort to teach their people how to treat the preacher. I do not think in so doing they do an injustice to the Scriptures. I do believe, however, that the pastor should pause to realize that the primary teaching of this verse deals with the way pastors should treat each other—not only pastors within the same church, but pastors of churches within the same community, state, nation, world, etc.

Concerning this subject, I always defend the pastor. When I hear something negative about a man of God, I do not believe it! When there is a battle between a pastor and laymen, I defend the pastor! I am not always right in this, but I am right more times than wrong, and I'm right more times than if I use my own judgment and intuition. It has been my policy through the years to defend God's man and God's men. Sometimes I have been proven wrong, but I have never been sorry for the policy.

I will not counsel or give an appointment to a member of another area fundamental church without a written note from the pastor of that church requesting that I counsel with his member.

I will not visit nor allow my staff or members to visit the home of the member of another fundamental church in the area. This is true even if this person brings his family to visit our services. This is also true even if he checks the little square at the bottom of the visitor's card, signifying that he is interested in joining First Baptist Church of Hammond. I am for God's men! I know they are not perfect, but I believe the finest group of men in the world is that group which composes God's men. I am glad that it is still news when one goes bad. This means that most do not!

Not only does God admonish us concerning the way the follower should treat the pastor and the way the pastors should treat each other, but it admonishes us concerning the way the pastor should treat the followers, or for that matter, the way any leader should treat any follower.

1. *The leader should give the same loyalty to the follower that he expects from the follower.* Much is said about loyalty from the bottom up. More should be said about loyalty from the top down. Oftentimes leaders come to me expressing their dismay and disdain because of disloyal followers. Loyalty, however, is a two-way street and should go from the leader to the follower as well as from the follower to the leader. This chapter is being written at the time of the Congressional hearings and the questioning of Colonel North, Admiral Poindexter, Mr. McFarland and others. I will not attempt to go into the pros and cons or to be provocative concerning these hearings, but concerning the matter of loyalty, I have been very impressed with the loyalty to each other by the men being questioned. Subordinates have appeared to be extremely loyal to leaders, and superiors have been extremely loyal, in my opinion, to subordinates. This is the way it should be.

2. *Leaders should accept followers as equals.* A man is not necessarily a leader because he is superior to someone else. A man is not necessarily a follower because he is inferior to another. The art of following is just as great as the art of leading, and a leader who expects loyal followers should be a loyal leader and should stand by his followers in the same manner that he expects his followers to stand by him. The leader should certainly not look

down from a pedestal to the follower, and he should respect the art of following as much as the follower respects the art of leading.

All of us are leaders and all of us are followers. This is as it should be. To be a good leader, one must be in some area of life a follower so he can know the heartbeat of the follower. To be a good follower, one must be in some area of life a leader so he can know the heartbeat of the leader. A man may be a leader at home, as he heads his family, and then a follower at work; or a man may be a leader at work and a follower at church, or a man may be a leader at work and a follower at work. Perhaps he is a foreman who has a superintendent for whom he works and laborers who work for him.

I have a wonderful man who works with me named Randy Ericson. Randy is in charge of the maintenance of the many buildings at First Baptist Church. He has several custodians who work for him, and Randy in turn works for me. When we come to church, I am the leader and Randy is the follower. When he takes me down to the boiler room to look at a problem in the heating system, he is the leader and I am the follower. There is no place in any organization for big shots and little shots. Everybody is important. All of us should look at the rest of us as equals.

3. *Each of us should purposely be followers in some area.* There is hardly a week that passes without my receiving a call from some pastor concerning trouble in his church. It is almost always the same trouble. Somebody in the church who is a leader everywhere else he goes wants to run the church and take the pastor's position. Here is a man who owns a business, is president of a civic club, a leader in politics, who comes to church. It is difficult for him to follow, but it is good for him to do so, because obedience is a quality that gives one the right to be a master. **Luke 15:25-32, "Now his elder son was in the field: and as he came and drew nigh to the house, he heard musick and dancing. And he called one of the servants, and asked what these things meant. And he said unto him, Thy brother is come; and thy father hath killed the fatted calf, because he hath received him safe and sound. And he was angry, and would not go in: therefore came his**

**father out, and intreated him. And he answering said to his father, Lo, these many years do I serve thee, neither transgressed I at any time thy commandment: and yet thou never gavest me a kid, that I might make merry with my friends: but as soon as this thy son was come, which hath devoured thy living with harlots, thou hast killed for him the fatted calf. And he said unto him, Son, thou art ever with me, and all that I have is thine. It was meet that we should make merry, and be glad: for this thy brother was dead, and is alive again; and was lost, and is found.''** This is the story about the brother of the prodigal son. This is the brother who stayed at home and worked for his father. Notice the two things that the son said in verse 29. What a wonderful pair of statements! Now notice later on in **verse 31** the father says, **"Son, all that I have is thine."** Note that the father said to the son that everything he had was his. How did the son get this mastery over his father? He got it because he said, **"Neither transgressed I at any time thy commandment."** He said, **"Dad, I never disobeyed you."** His dad said, **"Then all that I have is yours."** Obedience is the way to mastery. Obedience causes the one who is the servant to be the master over the one who is the served and makes the master a servant to the servant.

Obedience is the key that unlocks the door to authority. For example, I am now driving a car through the mountains of northern California. I got in the car and the car said to me, "Obey me. Put the key in the place prepared for it and turn the key to the right. If you will obey me, I will let you master me." Now I could have said to the car, "Nobody is going to tell me what to do. I don't believe in obedience." The car would have said to me, "Then you will never master me, for the way to master me is to obey me. You put the key where I say to put it and twist it like I say to twist it, and you may have me as your servant." I did this in obedience to the command of the car. Immediately I became master of the car. I am driving it now. I am turning to the right a little bit. I decide which way the car turns. I can play the radio if I want to. I can turn it down; I can turn it up; I can turn it on; I can turn it off. I can turn it to any station that I choose. I can turn on the air-conditioning. I can set it where I want to set it, or I can turn it off, or I can turn on the heater if I choose. I can turn on the outside lights, the inside lights, the parking lights, the flashing lights and do as I will. I can make the car go faster or slower, or I can stop it. I can turn it to the right or I can turn it to the left. How did I get this command over the car? By obeying. Obedience is the way to mastery.

A wall socket in the house says to me, "Obey me, and I will serve you." I say to the wall socket, "Nobody is going to tell me what to do." The wall socket says, "Then I will not give you my power." I finally decide to yield and obey the wall socket. When I do so, it will play a radio for me; it will operate an electric shaver, waffle iron, television, iron, washing machine, dishwasher, or whatever I decide. All I have to do is obey the wall socket, and then I become its master. Obedience is not the bad word that our generation has made it. It is the way to mastery, not the way to slavery.

Read Psalm 1:1-3, **"Blessed is the man that walketh not in the counsel of the ungodly, nor standeth in the way of sinners, nor sitteth in the seat of the scornful. But his delight is in the law of the Lord; and in His law doth he meditate day and night. And he shall be like a tree planted by the rivers of water, that bringeth forth his fruit in his season; his leaf also shall not wither; and whatsoever he doeth shall prosper."**

God gives us five things here that will make Him a servant to us. He says if we walk not in the counsel of the ungodly and do not stand in the way of sinners or sit in the seat of the scornful but delight in the law of the Lord and meditate therein day and night, He will see to it that we prosper. He says, "You do these five things in obedience to Me, and I will obey you."

**II Chronicles 7:14, "If My people, which are called by My name, shall humble themselves, and pray, and seek My face, and turn from their wicked ways; then will I hear from heaven, and will forgive their sin, and will heal their land."**

God says to us that if His people, called by His name, will humble themselves, pray, seek His face, turn from their wicked ways, that He will hear from Heaven, forgive their sins. He says, "If you will obey Me, I'll obey you. The way to mastery over Me is to obey Me."

**John 15:7, "If ye abide in Me, and My words abide in you, ye shall ask what ye will, and it shall be done unto you."** God says to us, "Abide in Me; let My words abide in you. Then I will obey you. Ask what ye will." God reminds us, **"Command ye Me."**

**Psalm 37:4, "Delight thyself also in the Lord; and He shall give thee the desires of thine heart."** God says, "Delight yourself in Me, and I'll give you the desires of your heart." Ah, what a blessed, blessed truth! Obedience is the way to mastery. Followship is the way to leadership, and no one should lead who hasn't followed; no one will lead successfully who has not followed; and no one can be a master until he has obeyed.

**Matthew 28:19, 20, "Go ye therefore, and teach all nations, baptizing them in the name of the Father, and of the Son, and of the Holy Ghost: teaching them to observe all things whatsoever I have commanded you: and, lo, I am with you alway, even unto the end of the world. Amen."** Notice the words in **verse 18, "All power is given unto Me in heaven and in earth."** This is followed by a command, **"Go, teach, baptize, and teach others."** These commands are followed by a promise, **"Lo, I am with you alway, even unto the end of the world."** What a blessed truth! He goes back to that "all power" before the commands. He says, "All power is given unto Me. I will give you that power and give you the right to have that power if you will obey Me. In other words, you obey Me, and you can be the master." Obedience is the way to mastery.

The earth says to the tree, "Obey me. Place in me your roots, and all of my wealth will come to your growth." The teacher says to the student, "Obey me, and all of my knowledge will be at your disposal." The parent says to the child, "Obey me, and all that I have can be yours," such as is seen in the story of the prodigal son's brother in Luke 15.

4. *The leader should try to learn the needs of each follower.* Bear

in mind that the leader has access to powers not accessible to the follower. These powers should be used in order to help the follower, so the leader should be very sensitive to the follower's needs.

5. *The leader should try to meet the needs of each follower.* What a blessed truth! Since the leader has the wherewithal that the follower often does not have, and since the leader is supposed to have discernment concerning the needs of the follower, he then should use that wherewithal to satisfy the needs that are known by his discernment.

6. *The leader should get ideas from the follower.* My definition of leadership perhaps is oversimplified, but here it is: A leader is one who goes to all of his followers to learn from them; he compiles a list of all he has learned and gives each follower a copy. As has been said, preaching is pouring back to the congregation in a flood what the congregation sends to the preacher in a vapor. Leading is collecting the knowledge of the followers and making each follower aware of the knowledge of all the rest.

I travel every week. I go to every part of the country. I learn everywhere I go, and then I take what I learn from each part of the country and try to teach those who look to me in some way as a leader.

7. *The leader should give strength to the follower.* This is much the same as the preaching. Each follower gives a little strength to the leader, making him stronger. The leader then uses this strength received from the followers to give strength and security to the followers who made him strong.

8. *The leader should be a servant of the follower.* Did not the Master say that the servant is greatest of all? The way that we become leaders and have the right to be leaders is by serving. In so serving he convinces his followers of his sincerity, concern, willingness and ability to lead. Coerced followship is dictatorship. Earned followship is leadership.

Earlier in this chapter mention was made about loyalty. Loyalty is one of the most misunderstood traits and graces. In concluding this chapter, I would like for you to consider the following about loyalty.

Loyalty is not the absence of disloyalty. It is a positive trait, not the absence of a negative one. In other word, a person is not necessarily loyal because he is not disloyal. There is some ground between loyalty and disloyalty. Perhaps we could say there is loyalty, aloyalty and disloyalty. Disloyalty criticizes, aloyalty is silent, but loyalty defends! Both loyalty and disloyalty are vocal. Aloyalty is silent. Loyalty never allows one word of criticism about the leader. It is complete defense and support. It not only never says, "Did you hear about . . .?" but also it does not listen to, "Did you hear about . . .?" It does not participate in criticism with the tongue or the ear. It does not give itself the satisfaction of criticizing nor does it give a sympathetic ear which gives others the satisfaction of criticizing.

Everyone cannot be talented; everyone can be loyal. Loyalty is one trait that is attainable by all. Disloyalty is the one trait that is not excusable! It is the unpardonable sin! It is the most detestable and deplorable trait that a follower can have. It has caused heart-break to many leaders. It has caused heartbreak to more followers. It has ruined the reputation of many leaders. It has ruined the character of many followers. To those who possess disloyalty, it has become a terminal cancer and professional suicide.

Loyalty is the complete support and defense of a leader. There are several reasons why it should be given.

1. *Respect for the work.* A few days ago I received a call from a pastor whose church operates a grade school and a high school. This pastor told me a sad story about his principal becoming disloyal. He had gone from class to class announcing his resignation and giving the reasons why he was leaving.

Many years ago this pastor bought some property and began a church. He cleared off the property with his own hands and with blood, sweat and toil. Over many years he had seen the church, under his leadership, grow to a membership of several thousand, while the school had grown to an enrollment of several hundred. The pastor then employed this principal. The pastor gave to the principal the buildings which he had helped to build with his own hands, pupils whom he had won to Christ, supplies and equipment purchased with money that he had raised and much of which he had sacrificially given. Hence, the principal assumed responsibility over children whom he had not won in buildings he had not built using equipment he had not purchased. He had no moral right to damage the work on the altar of his own hurt feelings. If and when he felt he could no longer work happily in the situation, he should have courteously resigned and never offered or listened to any criticism of the pastor.

2. *Respect for success.* When one is a follower to a successful leader, the very success of that leader should command loyalty. For example, I am on the board of the SWORD OF THE LORD, a weekly publication edited by Dr. Curtis Hutson. I have been on this board for many years. Now suppose that I disagree with Dr. Hutson on some issue. I feel and have always felt that as a member of the board I should prefer his feelings above my own. I have never edited a newspaper; he has been an editor for many years. His success measured by the one-third of a million subscribers, or by almost any other criterion, should lead the wise follower to have complete confidence in the wisdom of the leader.

It is amazing how that in this revolutionary generation young people who have never built a chicken coop rebel against master builders, who have never led a squad think they can lead an army, who have never had a savings account think they can run a bank, and who have never been a dog catcher think they can improve the presidency, have absolutely no respect for success!

At this writing I know of a young man who has just assumed the responsibility of becoming principal of a school operated by a church and led by a pastor who founded the school, was its first principal and has overseen the work for years. This young man who is fresh out of college feels that the diploma he holds in his hands has given him the right and equipment to know more about Christian education than this pastor of many years' experience. He is manifesting a disloyalty which is disgraceful. Someone in school should have taught him "Loyalty 131," and if for no other reason, this loyalty should be manifested because of respect for the success of the pastor. He should be seeking the pastor's counsel instead of shunning it. He should be asking for the pastor's counsel instead of abhorring it.

3. *Respect for knowledge.* There are some things that the leader knows that no one else can know. This not only pertains to facts, talent, etc., but it also pertains to knowledge of people and circumstances which he, for obvious reasons, cannot divulge to the followers. In other words, the follower does not always have all of the facts. There are some things that only a leader can know. Hence, it may appear to the follower that the leader is taking a wrong course of action, causing the follower to oppose him vehemently. However, if the follower knew the facts that the leader cannot divulge to him, he would no doubt arrive at the same conclusion to which the leader has arrived. This means that the follower should trust the leader even if his judgment seems unwise, realizing that the leader possesses many facts that only he knows and that if he, the follower, were acquainted with the entire case, he would probably arrive at the same conclusion.

If, for any reason, the follower cannot give this trust and confidence to the leader, he should never under any condition rebel or revolt. He should very quietly and ethically tiptoe out. He has no right whatsoever to talk to anyone about his differences with the leader, and he should leave without causing as much as a ripple on the water.

4. *Respect for the system.* To be sure, we are all human beings stranded on a planet whirling through space. Since there is no one here but us, we have to govern ourselves. This means we have to choose leaders who will govern us. This is why in our system a country has a king or a president, a state has a governor, a city has a mayor, a family has a father, a church has a pastor, and an employee has a boss. Someone must be at the top. The system itself should require loyalty from the follower to the leader. When this system breaks down, anarchy follows the breakdown, and chaos follows the anarchy. This is why we are reminded again and again in the Bible to respect our leaders, obey those who are over us and follow

those who lead us. Oftentimes the leader is not of God, but the system is of God and the position is of God. This is why God admonishes children to obey their parents, servants to obey their masters, wives to obey their husbands, citizens to obey their governments, etc. The system is God's plan. We must not rebel against it.

5. *Respect for your future.* Disloyal followers are seldom given loyal followers when they become leaders. Disloyal followers make poor leaders.

I have known hundreds of assistant pastors, music directors and education directors to be disloyal and to cause trouble in the church by trying to unseat the pastor or spread rumors about him. I have known very few who have won, and in practically every case, the damage to the disloyal follower is far greater than the damage to the criticized leader. Criticism always hurts the critic more than the criticized. Hatred always hurts the hater more than the hated. Gossip always hurts the gossiper more than the one about whom he gossips. The disloyal follower always stands to lose more than he takes from the accused leader.

There is also a law of sowing and reaping. In the Bible we are reminded that everything is reproduced after its own kind. Over and over again in the book of Genesis we find everything has in itself its own seed to bring forth its own kind. This is true not only in the physical but also in the emotional, in the personality and in the character. The pastor who criticizes other pastors will have people who criticize him. The teacher who criticizes the principal will have pupils who criticize him. God has a way of "letting our chickens come home to roost."

Not only does the subordinate usually lose, but he is also forming a habit of being disloyal that will hound him the rest of his life. Look at Abraham and Lot. Lot and his herdsmen became disloyal to Abraham. Lot chose for himself the best land, but look at the life of heartache that followed. I have lived long enough to see how battles turn out. I have watched young men become disloyal to leaders. I have watched these young men become middle-aged men. I have scrutinized their careers carefully. When as a follower one is disloyal, he is usually as a leader suspicious of those who work under him, for he has developed a life pattern which leads to failure and stifles success.

It has also been interesting through the years to watch the development of the children of disloyal people. It is interesting, tragic and almost unbelievable to see how disloyalty in the life of a parent affects the children. Through the years I have made surveys of the children of people who have become disloyal and have left churches that I have pastored. In not one case has a single child gone into full-time service for God, and in most cases, they have become adults who do not even attend church. A part of this is because of their secret and maybe even subconscious disgust for the disloyal parents. Part of it is because the kind of churches chosen later by these people does not turn out the best product. A part of it is God's judgment and the law of sowing and reaping doing its work.

6. *Respect for the unsaved.* When Abraham and Lot and their herdsmen had trouble, there is a statement which is brief but arresting which says simply, **"And the Canaanite and the Perizzite dwelled then in the land." (Genesis 13:7b)** In other words, others saw the strife. They heard the bickering. They observed the disloyalty. One wonders how many people will spend eternity in Hell because of disloyalty which results in bickering, gossip, slander, criticism, vindication, retaliation and other traits spawned in Hell by Lucifer and his angels.

# Chapter 7

# Treatment of Those Who Have Qualities That Are Irritating

Genesis 13:5-11, "And Lot also, which went with Abram, had flocks, and herds, and tents. And the land was not able to bear them, that they might dwell together: for their substance was great, so that they could not dwell together. And there was strife between the herdmen of Abram's cattle and the herdmen of Lot's cattle: and the Canaanite and the Perizzite dwelled then in the land. And Abram said unto Lot, Let there be no strife, I pray thee, between me and thee, and between my herdmen and thy herdmen; for we be brethren. Is not the whole land before thee? separate thyself, I pray thee, from me: if thou wilt take the left hand, then I will go to the right; or if thou depart to the right hand, then I will go to the left. And Lot lifted up his eyes, and beheld all the plain of Jordan, that it was well watered every where, before the Lord destroyed Sodom and Gomorrah, even as the garden of the Lord, like the land of Egypt, as thou comest unto Zoar. Then Lot chose him all the plain of Jordan; and Lot journeyed east: and they separated themselves the one from the other."

Romans 16:17, "Now I beseech you, brethren, mark them which cause divisions and offences contrary to the doctrine which ye have learned; and avoid them."

As is often said on these pages, faithful fundamentalist people are interwoven into a family-like situation for many hours a week. Now any two people who are closely associated will have qualities

61

that irritate each other. There are some people who leave a ring around the bathtub. Others leave the pickle jar lid unscrewed. Still others squeeze the toothpaste from the top of the tube. In our fundamental churches we are going to find habits and qualities in other people that are irritating to us. In our effort to keep peace, we must find ways to prevent this irritation. Of necessity, this happens in homes, churches, jobs, school and at play. In order for peace to prevail and unity to reign, this problem must be solved, as follows:

1. *Do not rely on doing better.* Especially is this true in the case of adults. Fire and gasoline will always explode when united. The gasoline can vow to do better, and the fire can promise to improve, but it will not be done; explosion is inevitable. Oil and water will never mix. Oil may promise to mix with water, and water may make a resolution to mix with oil, but they will never mix. Because of this, it is usually best for other measures to be taken.

2. *Discover what it is about you that irritates your friend and what it is about your friend that irritates you.* Face it with frank reality.

3. *Stay away from circumstances that cause this irritation.* Abraham was Lot's uncle. When Abraham left the Ur of the Chaldees, he took his nephew with him and reared him as if he were his own son. When a famine came in the land, Abraham took his family to Egypt. There he and Lot both became wealthy, and as is often the case, their wealth caused problems between them. Their employees began to war with each other. Something had to be done! Abraham approached Lot and suggested that Lot choose whatever land he wanted for himself. Abraham then agreed to take what was left. He was simply saying, "Lot, let's not allow strife between us. Let us alleviate that which causes the strife. It is best that we not own the same land and share the same property. Let us circumvent the circumstances that cause the friction and the things that are irritants to each of us. In other words, let us stay away from what irritates us and causes us trouble."

There are some people that you can work with, but you cannot play with them. In such cases, do work together, but do not play together.

Then there are some people with whom you can play but with whom you cannot work. In such cases, have social life with them, but do not bear the yoke of work together.

There are some people that you can be with for a short time but not for a long time. To be together for awhile is pleasant and delightful, but after awhile irritation comes. In such cases, discover how long you can be together before a problem arises, and limit yourself to that amount of time.

There are some people with whom certain subjects cause strife and stress. In such cases, avoid those subjects. Recently I was fellowshipping with a young man. We probably agree on most everything, but there is one subject about which we cannot agree. We were having a wonderful time. Then he brought up the subject. I suggested that since we were having such a good time together we not allow ourselves to enter into an area where we disagree. He agreed that we should stay within the boundaries of those things and not to enter into that subject which would cause us irritation.

There are certain people who make certain statements that irritate us. Discover those statements and avoid them. Far too many of us want to irritate each other, and at certain times in order to do so, we will use statements that we know will cause friction.

I know one man who, when he is angry at his wife, inevitably uses the statement, "You are just like your mother!" He knows that that statement will hurt his wife, and when he wants to hurt her, he uses it. Why should any of us want to hurt any of the rest of us! In order for churches to stay united, its members need to use extra care not to say things that will cause another to hurt.

There are some people who work better when communication is by memo, and there are others who work better when communication is by conversation. The wise person will learn the preferences of his friend and act wisely.

There are some things that two people cannot share. The wise people will discover them and avoid them. Years ago when our children were small, Mrs. Hyles and I took the children to visit their maternal grandparents. At that time we lived only about 20 miles from them, and one night a week we went over to their house for a meal. One evening while we were there, I became a little nauseated. I went to Mrs. Hyles' mother, whom we call MaMaw Slaughter, and said, "MaMaw, I'm not feeling well. Do you have any Alka Seltzer?"

She said that she did not.

I said, "I always thought you kept Alka Seltzer."

She said, "Well, I'm out now." I don't know why, but I had some suspicion that she was not telling me the truth. A while later I was in the kitchen and I saw a bottle of Alka Seltzer on the windowsill. I went to the other room and told MaMaw. I reminded her that I had asked her if she had any Alka Seltzer and that she had told me that she had not. Then I told her that I had seen those in the kitchen.

She replied, "Oh, those are PaPaw's (her husband's)." I then learned that they had had some disagreement about how tight the lid should be placed on Alka Seltzer bottles, so in order to prevent being irritated with each other, they had decided that each would have his own bottle of Alka Seltzers.

At first thought, one may think that this is being a little picky, but I like it! They did not want to fuss or irritate each other. They had found one area that caused friction, and they had circumvented that area. They detoured around the Alka Seltzers in order to avoid tension between themselves.

When our children were small, Mrs. Hyles and I had some difference of opinion in how we should discipline them. (Of course, I was right!) This could have caused real friction, but we detoured around the friction and agreed that when one of us was disciplining the children, the other would leave the room. Many times one of us would be disciplining the children and the other would take a walk around the block or go out in the yard for a few minutes. This kept me from having to witness her excessive leniency, and it kept her from having to witness the execution when I was the disciplinarian.

There are some people who are strongly opinionated. Occasionally two such people marry or two such people share the same bus route or are on the same staff. When strongly-opinionated people share in the same work, it is usually best for the opinion not to be expressed. Once again, we are circumventing areas of friction and tension.

It is usually best for people who are together a lot not to speak often of ailments. To most people, constant complaining about a headache, a toothache, weariness, etc. is irritating. If such is the case, people would be wise to suffer alone rather than to fight together. The wise people will find those conditions, circumstances and habits that gender strife between them and avoid them.

The wise teacher will eliminate the exposure of unnecessary things that are irritating to the students. Likewise, the wise husband, wife, father, mother, son, daughter, coach, athlete, pastor, staff members, employer, employee and friends in all areas of life will be careful to avoid those events, times, subjects, activities and words which can do nothing but harm.

Maybe the couple should have two Alka Seltzer bottles or two ketchup bottles. Perhaps they should agree not to watch the other discipline the children. Care should be taken to find the things that are irritating. Ask each other. Be frank with each other. Instead of scolding one another because of an idiosyncrasy and instead of giving accusations of stubbornness, why not try to avoid the things that irritate?

To be sure, there should be a constant effort by both parties to correct the things that cause a problem, but until that correction is complete, the irritants should be avoided. This is what Abraham did.

# Chapter 8

# Treatment of Your Friends' Enemies

Let it be established first, however, that kindness should be exerted to everybody, but let it also be established that though we are not to defend ourselves when attacked, we are, however, to defend our friends when they are attacked. This is to be done only in defense of our friends.

1. *You will not criticize my friend in my presence.* In fact, I will ask you not to be critical at all in my presence, but I definitely will not remain with you if you are criticizing my friend. I will ask you to cease the criticism, or I will remove myself from your presence.

Several years ago I was sharing a taxicab with a well-known preacher who began to criticize my friend, John R. Rice. Immediately I asked the taxi driver to stop, and in plain words I defended my friend and warned his attacker.

I was prevailed upon in a southern city to eat out after a service one night. The pastor, the other guest speaker, the guest soloist, two of my friends and I were sitting around the table when suddenly the singer spoke an unkind word about one of my friends who was not present. Immediately I said, "That isn't so! You are talking about my friend, and he isn't that kind of a person, and I will not sit here and listen to you attack him!" I will not retaliate if you attack me, but I will not allow you in my presence to attack those whom I love.

2. *I will not socialize with the enemies of my friends.* I will not be unkind to them as long as they sheathe their swords, but I will not

socialize with them. I will feed them if they are hungry; I will clothe them if they are cold; I will put shoes on their bare feet, but I will not socialize with them. I do not require my friends to follow the same policy, nor do I ask my friends to assume my enemies, but my irrevocable policy is to love those who are enemies to my friends, to help them if they need help, but not to enter into a social time with them.

For many years Dr. John Rice and I traveled often together. We shared pulpits across America at least once a month, sometimes twice a month, and on rare occasions three or four times a month. I was his friend.

For a number of years we had preached together at the same church. Then the time came when the pastor made an attack against Dr. Rice. The pastor was a good man and his attack was not vicious, but nevertheless, it was an attack. Dr. Rice was no longer welcome to preach in his pulpit. Because of this, I refused to return to that church when I was invited the next time. The pastor asked for my reason. I explained to him that John Rice is my friend, and that if he did not choose to have John Rice, I would still come; but when he chooses to attack John Rice and then decide not to have him again, I would not come. I explained to him that this policy would be in effect until such time when he would have Dr. Rice and me come back together for a meeting. To the credit of that good man, not many months passed until he realized what he should do. He wrote me and told me that he would have Dr. Rice to return. Dr. Rice and I did return to his church and preach together again. From that day until the day that John Rice went to Heaven, he and this pastor were dear friends. Now I never chose to fight this beloved pastor, nor did I explain to anyone anywhere the position that I was taking. I certainly did not become his enemy; I just simply could not preach in his pulpit until his attack against my friend was withdrawn and reconciliation was sought. If, during this time, this dear pastor would have had a need of which I knew, I would have been among the first to come to his side, but I would not have socialized with him because I wanted my friendship to be obvious to my friend.

Maybe Peter was right when he rose to the defense of Jesus at the time of betrayal, and certainly Jesus was right when he replaced the ear of his enemy.

Several years ago one of our parking lot attendants was helping park cars in the church parking lot. It was the evening of the Hammond Baptist High School commencement exercises. A guest got out of his car and, while walking past the attendant, cursed me. My parking lot attendant instinctively "decked" the man. Now I told my friend that he shouldn't have done what he did, but under my breath I couldn't help but smile a bit—not because I wanted someone hurt, but because I appreciated the zeal of my friend in defending his pastor, even though his zeal was perhaps somewhat misguided.

Maybe Abishai was right when he drew his sword in defense of his friend King David, and certainly David was right when he told Abishai to sheathe his sword.

3. *When both the attacker and the attacked are my friends and I am theirs, I defend the accused.* Jonathan was certainly a loyal son to his father, King Saul. He was likewise a loyal friend to David. When King Saul attacked David, Jonathan was not defending David against Saul; he was defending the attacked. I have no doubt in my mind but that had David attacked Saul, Jonathan would have defended Saul as quickly as he defended David when Saul had attacked him.

I have many wonderful staff members, and have had many wonderful people work for me through these 40 years of pastoring. Occasionally, however, one of my staff members will become critical of another staff member. I always defend the one who is the accused. I do not know if the accused has done what the accuser said he did, so I do not know of the innocence or guilt of the accused. However, I DO know of the guilt of the accuser, because it is wrong to accuse.

I was preaching on the subject of false accusations. During the message I reminded my people that if they falsely accuse someone, they are doing the work of the Devil, because he is a false accuser, when suddenly a truth hit me of which I had never thought before! The Devil is not a false accuser; he is a true accuser! He accuses me to God and tells Him of my weaknesses, and what he says is true. So, when I enter into true accusation, I am wrong and I am entering into the work of the evil one.

I was in a hotel room with two of my preacher friends—both are well-known, famous preachers. They asked me if I had heard rumors about a certain preacher who also was well-known and famous. I immediately answered that I had not heard such rumors and that I would not listen to them, and I defended the absent brother vigorously. To the credit of the two men who were being critical, they both apologized and admitted that their words were unwise, and they vowed not to speak them again.

I was in a certain city preaching. As soon as the pastor and I got in the car to leave the airport, he began to tell me of a friend who had gone astray. Before he could tell me what had happened, I requested that he refrain from doing so. He insisted on telling me. I asked him then to stop the car and let me out. I told him that I was going to take the next plane right back to Chicago, and that I was not going to listen to criticism of my friend.

Quite often when I am preaching somewhere, a layman in the church will approach me about his pastor. Not only do I defend the pastor, but I will not listen to the criticism.

In summary, I am not to fight my enemy; I am to love him, pray for him, bless him and do good to him. I will assume my friends' enemies, though I will not require them to do the same to mine. If the accused is my friend and the accuser is my friend, and I am the friend of both, I will defend the accused. I will not socialize with enemies of my friends, though I will be unkind to no one.

# Chapter 9

# Treatment of Enemies (1)

### A Sermon Preached on a Sunday Evening at the First Baptist Church of Hammond, Indiana

Mark 8:27-33, "And Jesus went out, and His disciples, into the towns of Caesarea Philippi: and by the way He asked His disciples, saying unto them, Whom do men say that I am? And they answered, John the Baptist: but some say, Elias; and others, One of the prophets. And He saith unto them, But whom say ye that I am? And Peter answereth and saith unto Him, Thou art the Christ. And He charged them that they should tell no man of Him. And He began to teach them, that the Son of man must suffer many things, and be rejected of the elders, and of the chief priests, and scribes, and be killed, and after three days rise again. And He spake that saying openly. And Peter took Him, and began to rebuke Him. But when He had turned about and looked on His disciples, He rebuked Peter, saying, Get thee behind me, Satan: for thou savourest not the things that be of God, but the things that be of men."

Matthew 26:47-50, "And while He yet spake, lo, Judas, one of the twelve, came, and with him a great multitude with swords and staves, from the chief priests and elders of the people. Now he that betrayed Him gave them a sign, saying, Whomsoever I shall kiss, that same is He: hold Him fast. And forthwith he came to Jesus, and saith, Hail, master; and kissed Him. And Jesus said unto him, Friend, wherefore art thou come? Then came they, and laid hands on Jesus, and took Him."

## To My Enemies of Forty Years

**"And whosoever shall compel thee to go a mile, go with him twain. Give to him that asketh thee, and from him that would borrow of thee turn not thou away. Ye have heard that it hath been said, Thou shalt love thy neighbour, and hate thine enemy. But I say unto you, Love your enemies, bless them that curse you, do good to them that hate you, and pray for them which despitefully use you, and persecute you; that ye may be the children of your Father which is in heaven: for He maketh His sun to rise on the evil and on the good, and sendeth rain on the just and on the unjust. For if ye love them which love you, what reward have ye? do not even the publicans the same? And if ye salute your brethren only, what do ye more than others? do not even the publicans so? Be ye therefore perfect, even as your Father which is in heaven is perfect." (Matthew 5:41-48)**

Tonight I want to speak on a very unusual subject. I want to speak on the subject, "To My Enemies of Forty Years." I want you to think of your enemies as I think of those people who for forty years have come and gone and been enemies of this preacher.

"Our Heavenly Father, I pray tonight You would help us to enter into New Testament Christianity. Help us to be Christians in the New Testament sense. Give us, I pray, the attention of all the people tonight. Amen."

Tonight I would like to address a group of people that are scattered across many miles, people I'm sure some of whom live in every state of the union. Tonight I would like to address a group of people who are not only scattered across many miles but across many years. Forty years as a preacher of the Gospel I have lived with the awareness that some people hate me. I have lived with the awareness that this hatred is nationwide and almost in every state of the union. Tonight I would like to address those who are my enemies, not those who are in this room. No preacher has more people who are kind and gracious to him than I do! I do not feel at all that the people in this room need what I am going to say, but I was in east Texas recently, and I got to thinking while I was there for a couple of days about my young ministry and I got to thinking about some of the people in east Texas who are my enemies. As I flew into the Dallas–Fort Worth airport, I got to looking down and thinking of people in the great Dallas–Fort Worth area who were my enemies. Tonight I would like to address all of those people who for forty years have been my enemies. Some will hear me from Heaven. Others will hear me on tape as they hear this sermon played. Still others will hear by word of mouth, and maybe perchance, there are some in this room tonight.

What I will say tonight can be summarized by these words: I thank God for my enemies! I thank God for those who for all these years have been my enemies. No, I do not say that I enjoy having enemies, and I think it is easier thanking God for my friends, and I do thank God for my friends. No one has been blessed with as many close, dear precious friends as this preacher. Nobody has ever pastored a church of people who are more thoughtful than are the people of this church, and no preacher ever hears the words, "I love you," or reads the words, "I love you," more than I do. No preacher has a finer group of people.

Not only do I have many wonderful friends in this church, but all over America and all over the world God has given me a group of people who love me and who are my friends. Almost everywhere I go people say, "Look at all that hair!" and words of affection and "hurt." Almost everywhere I go, people walk up and say, "Show us your muscle," and some even say, "Reverend Boopsie-Woopsie!" It is almost cultish. I mean by that, there is almost a loyalty around the nation of literally hundreds of thousands of people to this church. This church is the headquarters of fundamentalism in America. I mean old-fashioned, Hell-fire and brimstone, rock-rib, black-is-black, white-is-white, the Bible is the Word of God, **"Ye must be born again,"** separated-from-the-world fundamentalism! This church is the headquarters of it in this nation. No doubt about it! People look to us. I thank God tonight, not only for the dear friends that I have here for whom and with whom I have labored these many years, but I thank God tonight for that great legion of friends all over the nation and around the world.

Tonight, however, I want to turn from that crowd of loyal people who love me. I want to thank God tonight for another group of people. I want to thank God for my enemies for these forty years. I speak to you as a group—you in Heaven, and I think there are a few of you who didn't quite make it! I thank God tonight for my enemies. Now I speak to all of you—both to you who hear me from Heaven, to you who hear me on tape and perchance to you who hear me in this room tonight, though I do not know who you are.

At first you surprised me. I did not know in those early days that you existed. I wasn't expecting you. I'll be quite frank with you, when I entered the ministry I did not know that preachers had enemies. I was a young man. I was naive. I remember when the first of you came to me in east Texas, I did not know how to react. I did not know the Scriptures, **"Love your enemies, bless them that curse you, do good to them that hate you, and pray for them which despitefully use you." "Whosoever shall smite thee on thy right cheek, turn to him the other also." "If any man take away thy coat, let him have thy cloke also."** I did not know these Scriptures. I'll be quite frank with you. In those early days I did not know the Scriptural way to react to you, my enemies. I'm afraid in those early days I often fought you back, and I'm sorry. I'm afraid in those early days I even preached against you from the pulpit, and I'm sorry. I'm afraid in those early days I did not turn the other cheek, and I'm sorry. I'm afraid in those early days I did not bless you when you cursed me, and I'm sorry. I'm afraid in those early days I did not love you when you hated me, and I'm sorry. I'm afraid in those early days I did not pray for you when you despitefully used me, and I'm sorry.

The other day I was asked at a question-answer session, "Dr. Hyles, if you had your life to live over again, can you think of any changes you'd make?"

I said quickly, "Yes, I can think of one. If I had my life to live over again I'd like to take back some of the things I said to my enemies many years ago. I would like to take back some of the things I did to my enemies many years ago. If I had my life to live over, I would like to live over some of those days when I did not know that the Bible teaches me to love those that hate me, to do good to those that do evil to me, to bless those that curse me, and to pray for those that despitefully use me. If I had my life to live over, I'd like to live over the early days of my ministry when I retaliated, when I sought revenge. I was sincere; God knows that I was, but I did not understand it, and so I'd like to say this tonight to my enemies of over 40 years of my ministry: I have not always enjoyed you, but tonight I thank God for you.

Thank you for hating me, for had you not hated me I could never have obeyed God's command to love those that hate me. Thank you for cursing me, for had you not cursed me I could not have obeyed the command of God to bless those that curse me. Thank you for despitefully using me, for had you not despitefully used me, I could not have prayed for those who despitefully use me. Thank you for smiting me, my enemies, for had you not smitten me, I could not have turned the other cheek. Thank you for taking my coat, for had you not taken my coat I could not have heeded the admonition of the Scripture, **"If any man take away thy coat, let him have thy cloke also."** Thank you for making me go a mile, for had you not forced me to go a mile, I could not have gone two miles with you. May I say this. That is what I've done for 24 years. I have not always turned the other cheek, but I have for 24 years. I have not always blessed those that curse me, but I have for 24 years. I have not always loved those that hated me, but I have for 24 years. I am not lying to you. I'd rather die now than lie behind the sacred desk. I may sometimes tell you something that's not true, but not to my knowledge. I would rather die tonight than to stand behind this pulpit and tell you something that isn't true. I say this tonight with one hand on this Book and my heart laid bare—for 24 years I have not had bitterness in my heart toward anybody. For 24 years I have not hated anybody. For 24 years I have tried to love those that hate me, I have prayed for those that despitefully use me, and I have blessed those that curse me. I do not claim to have apprehended. I do not claim even to be a good Christian, but I do say this: On my face in a little hospital room in Dyer, Indiana, when our little girl

Linda was at the brink of death, I got on my knees and I promised God that I would love my enemies from that day until this.

Tonight I want to thank my enemies. I want to thank God for you because you have caused me to have the opportunity to obey the command of my Lord in my relationship with you. I'm sorry that before 24 years ago I often smote you back. I'm sorry that before 24 years ago I maybe wanted to smite you back. I'm sorry for the six months of bitterness I had toward you when I was about 30 years of age. In one of the darkest hours of my life when I thought my ministry was gone, I became bitter, and for six months of my life bitterness filled my soul when I was about 30 years of age. I apologize tonight to my enemies for allowing bitterness to come into my heart, because if I'm bitter toward you, it is not you who loses; it is I who lose! If I shoot you, the bullet boomerangs and hits me also. I am sorry that on occasion when you hated me, I hated you. I am sorry that on occasion when you wronged me, I wronged you. I am sorry that on occasion when you did me evil, I did you evil back.

From the moment 24 years ago I knelt in Dyer Mercy Hospital on the third floor of a little dark hospital room and said, "Dear God, take this bitterness out of my heart," until this moment, I have never harbored bitterness in my heart toward anybody, and there is not a human who lives tonight—not a one—but if he stabs me in the breast I'll take the knife and give it back to him and buy him a new knife if he needs it. There is not a man in this world whom I wouldn't feed tonight if he were hungry. There is not a person living tonight whom I would not clothe if he were naked. There is not a person living tonight whom I would not help if he needed help.

I'm simply saying tonight—thank God for my enemies, for I would not have known to love you if I had not had you. I could not have turned the other cheek had you not smitten one. I could not have blessed you had you not cursed me. There is no preacher alive who is criticized more than I am. I do not know why. Maybe it's because of the size of the church; I do not know why. I refuse tonight to live with revenge in my heart. I refuse tonight to live with

vengeance in my soul. I refuse tonight to curse those that curse me
and hate those that hate me. I refuse! I cannot make you love me,
but you cannot keep me from loving you. I wish I could show you
my heart. I often feel when I am preaching around the country that I
would like to take this little pocket knife which I always carry (I'm
a Switchblader from Hammond City Baptist High School) and cut
my heart open and let you see it. You would find a heart of love.
That's the truth. My sword is sheathed. My tongue is bridled. My
guns are stacked. My arsenal is empty. My quiver is bare.

I speak to my enemies all over the world tonight. I cannot
criticize you, and I will not knowingly hurt you. If I had David's
sword at the cave where thou art sleeping, I would not smite thee. In
these 24 years I have not allowed others to speak ill of thee in my
presence. I have not asked my friends to shun thee. I desire my
friends to be your friends, even though you are my enemy. I do not
say that you are all bad because you are my enemies. No doubt I
have on occasion deserved you. Perhaps I have left the wrong
impression at times, or perhaps you did not totally understand. And
though I have never wanted you to be my enemy, I have always
needed you. Without thee, I would not have known God as well.
You have allowed me to spend more time with Him and for us to get
to know each other better. You have taught me to love those that
hate me. Thank you for teaching me. You have taught me to pray for
those that despitefully use me. You have taught me to bless those
that curse me. Thank you for making it possible. I am grateful.
Though I have not totally been able to rejoice and be exceeding
glad as I am commanded to in the Scriptures, I am grateful, and I
love you.

If you desire an enemy, you must look elsewhere. If you desire a
fight, I will not oblige you. If you hate me, I will love you back, and
you can't keep me from it! You curse me, and I will bless you back,
and you can't keep me from it. You take my coat, and I'll give you
my cloke, and you can't keep me from it. You smite me, and I'll turn
the other cheek, and you can't keep me from it.

You say, Preacher, how is this possible? How is it possible for you to speak to hordes of enemies over 40 years around the world and say to people that hate you, "I love you"? How could you say to people that curse you, "I'll bless you"? How could you say to people who despitefully use you, "I'll pray for you"? How could you say to people who have smitten your cheek, "I'll turn the other cheek"? How could you sheathe your sword and stack your arms and bridle your tongue and empty your arsenal and bare your quiver? How could you do it?

This is how. You see, I once did evil to a Man myself. I once took a hammer and drove nails into a Man's hands. You have not done to me what I've done to a Man. I once said, "Crucify Him! Crucify Him!" I once delivered Him to the hands of an angry mob. I once placed the kiss of betrayal on His brow. I once stood and warmed my feet by the fire and followed from afar as they took the lovely Lord away to Calvary. I took the cat-o'-nine tails in my hand and beat His back beyond recognition. I joined the crowd that said, "Release Barabbas! Release Barabbas! Crucify Jesus! Crucify Him! Crucify Him!" My voice joined that crowd, and my sin put Him naked at the mercy of the scourges. I held the coats of those who nailed His hands and feet to the cross. I put nails in His hands. I put nails in His feet. I put a crown of thorns on His brow. I put a spear in His side. I mocked Him, treated Him as a mock king and put a sign over Him that said, "THIS IS THE KING OF THE JEWS!" I did it, and while I did it, He opened His mouth and said, "Father, forgive them; for they know not what they do."

If He Who knew no sin could forgive me who is sin, I can forgive you, my brother sinner. If He Whose feet never walked a crooked path, Whose mind never had an evil thought, Whose hands never did an evil deed, Whose heart never had an evil motive, Whose lips never spoke an evil word, if He after I have crucified Him could say, "Father forgive him, he knows not what he does," I do not understand to save my life why those of us sinners saved by His grace have to harbor ill will toward each other.

But He did more than that! He forgave me, and He justified me! He pronounced me as if I had never sinned, and though I was a part and parcel in crucifying Him, and though these hands drove nails in His and though this tongue and this sin from body, life, heart and mind put Him on the cross, not only did He forgive me, but when I trusted Him, He erased from His judicial record in glory every sin I ever committed!

"I'm justified! I'm happy in Jesus today.
The sins I've committed, they're all in the past;
They've all been forgiven, and He holds me fast!
I'm justified! I'm justified!
I'm happy in Jesus today."

That isn't all He did! Not only did He forgive me, and not only did He justify me, but He saved me! He wrote my name in the Book of Life! He delivered me from the fires of Hell! Tonight He is preparing a home in the Gloryland, where I can live forever, not because I am righteous, for I am not! I am unrighteous! I'm a sinner saved by His grace, forgiven by His love, justified by His justice, saved by His mercy, redeemed by His blood, indwelt by His Spirit, led by His Word, saved by His Son and headed for Heaven by His amazing grace! I didn't deserve a bit of it! You are looking tonight at a man who deserves to go to Hell. I am looking at thousands of folks tonight who deserve to burn in Hell. I don't understand it. If He could forgive us after all we've done to Him, then we ought to forgive each other for what mistakes others have made toward us.

I always wanted to go to the Holy Land. (Not many folks want to go now—they're chicken!) I always wanted to go to the place where they took His little body and wrapped it in swaddling clothes and laid Him in a manger. I always wanted to go to the place where He knelt and prayed on the mountain. I always wanted to go to the place where He was baptized in Jordan. I always wanted to go to the place where He turned the water into wine. I always wanted to go to the place where He fed the 5,000. I always wanted to go to the place where He was tried wrongly in Pilate's Hall. I always wanted to go to the place where He was crucified—Calvary! I always wanted to see the empty tomb! (I did see, and the tomb is empty!) I always wanted to go. I dreamed of going. Finally one year we got to go. We went the first time with a Bob Jones tour. There were about 23 of us, I think, on the tour. We stopped in Paris, but I wanted to see Calvary. We stopped in Rome, but I wanted to see Calvary. We stopped in Greece, but I wanted to see Calvary. We saw the Parthenon, but I wanted to see Calvary. We saw Corinth, but I wanted to see Calvary. We saw the Colosseum, but I wanted to see Calvary. We saw the catacombs, but I wanted to see Calvary. We went to Egypt and saw the pyramids, but I wanted to see Calvary. We saw the tombs of the kings, but I wanted to see Calvary. We saw the museum of Egypt with King Tut's possessions displayed, but I wanted to see Calvary. We saw the sphinx, but I wanted to see Calvary. We went to the Promised Land. I walked one day where Jesus walked. We saw the place where He was baptized, and I baptized several people in the Jordan River while a crowd on the bank sang, "On Jordan's stormy banks I stand and cast a wishful eye, to Canaan's fair and happy land where my possessions lie." We went to the Sea of Galilee. We saw that hill where He preached His sermon to the 5,000 and multiplied the loaves and fishes and fed them miraculously. We saw the synagogue in Capernaum, where Peter attended when he was growing up. We went to Bethlehem and sang, "O little town of Bethlehem, how still we see thee lie!"

Then one day we went to Calvary! It is a little place. There is a bus station now at the bottom of that little hill, but there was none there then. It is a hill that looks just like a face. It is sort of an embankment. It is not very high. I do not think it is as high as this auditorium. On top there is a cemetery. There are layers of stone, and you can see two places that probably represent sunken eyes and a place that looks like a mouth and the place above the eyes that looks like the place of a skull. We knelt. I had always dreamed of kneeling there.

I had sung as a child, "Years I spent in vanity and pride, caring not my Lord was crucified, knowing not it was for me He died on Calvary." I had sung, "On a hill far away, stood an old rugged cross, the emblem of suffering and shame." I had sung, "At the cross, at the cross, where I first saw the light, and the burden of my heart rolled away," and finally I was there! I looked at Calvary, weeping uncontrollably! People left, but I couldn't leave! I was there alone! All of our crowd had gone back and gotten on the bus, but I couldn't go! That is where it happened! That is where my sin debt was paid! That is where my Saviour died! That's it! I began to sing and cry and cry and sing!

I can still see Dr. Bob Jones, Jr., coming back a little upset with me. He said, "Dr. Hyles, we've got to go! Everyone is waiting on you!"

I said, "I can't go yet! I can't go yet!"

I told that story once, and someone asked me what I was thinking about as I looked at Calvary. This is what I said: "I thought, 'If He could do that for me, I don't ever want to hate anybody again as long as I live! I don't ever want to speak unkindly about anybody as long as I live!' "

Ladies and gentlemen, you have enemies like I have. There are those who would do you ill, and those who have and will try to do you ill, but my Bible tells me to love them, and your Bible tells you to love them. My Bible tells me to bless them, and your Bible tells you to bless them. My Bible tells me to pray for them, and your Bible tells you to pray for them.

I wish tonight every person in this room could lie down to rest and sing, "Nothing between my soul and the Saviour, naught of this world's delusive dream."

# Chapter 10

# Treatment of Enemies (2)

In an institution as complex in its program as the fundamental New Testament church (which is composed of frail humanity) it is almost impossible for one to escape the distasteful position of having enemies. As we mingle within this little society within a society called the New Testament church, most if not all of us will accrue people who are our enemies. Though the sermon that you have just read covers much of the information and method of dealing with such people, it is perhaps wise that we enlarge at least somewhat upon it.

**Romans 12:14, "Bless them which persecute you: bless, and curse not."**

**Romans 12:17-21, "Recompense to no man evil for evil. Provide things honest in the sight of all men. If it be possible, as much as lieth in you, live peaceably with all men. Dearly beloved, avenge not yourselves, but rather give place unto wrath: for it is written, Vengeance is mine; I will repay, saith the Lord. Therefore if thine enemy hunger, feed him; if he thirst, give him drink: for in so doing thou shalt heap coals of fire on his head. Be not overcome of evil, but overcome evil with good."**

**Matthew 5:43-47, "Ye have heard that it hath been said, Thou shalt love thy neighbour, and hate thine enemy. But I say unto you, Love your enemies, bless them that curse you, do good to them that hate you, and pray for them which de-**

spitefully use you, and persecute you; that ye may be the children of your Father which is in heaven: for He maketh His sun to rise on the evil and on the good, and sendeth rain on the just and on the unjust. For if ye love them which love you, what reward have ye? do not even the publicans the same? And if ye salute your brethren only, what do ye more than others? do not even the publicans so?"

I Corinthians 6:7, "Now therefore there is utterly a fault among you, because ye go to law one with another. Why do ye not rather take wrong? why do ye not rather suffer yourselves to be defrauded?"

From these and other passages we arrive at the following conclusions:

1. *We are to love those that hate us.* What a perfect example of this our Saviour left for us! He has been scourged by the cat-o'-nine-tails. His body has been beaten beyond recognition. He has been wrongly tried. He has been nailed to a cross. He has been the object of jeers, profanity, hatred, malice and unbelievable persecution and suffering. He opens His mouth from the cross and what are His first words? "Father, forgive them; for they know not what they do." What a tremendous example of loving those who hated Him! The Scriptures plainly teach us that we are to be like Him.

I John 4:17, "Herein is our love made perfect, that we may have boldness in the day of judgment: because as He is, so are we in this world."

John 14:12, "Verily, verily, I say unto you, He that believeth on Me, the works that I do shall he do also; and greater works than these shall he do; because I go unto My Father."

Philippians 2:5, "Let this mind be in you, which was also in Christ Jesus."

John 20:21, "Then said Jesus to them again, Peace be unto you: as My Father hath sent Me, even so send I you."

In order to be like Him, we must grow to the place in our Christian lives where we love those that hate us. In other words, though we cannot avoid having enemies, we are to be no man's enemy. In other words, though people are offended toward us, we are to be offended toward no one. The Psalmist tells us, **"Great peace have they which love Thy law: and nothing shall offend them." (Psalm 119:165)**

2. *We are not to retaliate.* **Romans 12:14, 17-21.** Vengeance is the Lord's. He will care for that which is necessary. However, the spiritual Christian will not want vengeance to be given to his enemy unless the vengeance that God executes is for the enemy's good. In other words, we should not want the enemy to suffer because he has made us to suffer, unless that suffering can help him. At any rate, we are to leave that vengeance in the hands of God.

3. *We are to bless those that curse us and do good to those who do evil to us.* This admonishes us to actively do good to those who are our enemies. In other words, deeds and acts of kindness should be showered upon those who hate us. It may be that such deeds and acts must be done anonymously, but nevertheless, they should be done. We should never fight malice with malice. We should not use the methods of the demons to fight the demons. Our weapons are spiritual ones. We are to fight hatred with love, selfishness with unselfishness, cursing with blessing, greed with generosity, un-kindness with kindness, criticism with prayer, and bad with good.

This author is far from perfect, neither has he yet apprehended, but I can honestly say that for 24 years I have not had bitterness in my heart toward any human being, and for those 24 years I have loved my enemies. The lesson I learned was a hard one and a costly one. When I was pastoring in Garland, Texas, I was a young man, and the growth of the church had perhaps exceeded my ability to handle the situation properly.

There was a man in the church with whom I shared some unkind words. Some were spoken from me to him and some from him to me. I allowed a bad spirit toward him to enter into my heart and mind. He left the church and, to be quite frank, we would not speak to each other. Not long after that, I was called to pastor the First Baptist Church of Hammond. For about three years it seemed that the church could not get moving. Of course, I was not willing to admit the fact that at least part of the cause and blame should be laid at my feet because of my feelings toward the aforementioned man. One morning we took our little girl, Linda, who at the time was four years old, to the Mercy Hospital in Dyer, Indiana, for what we thought would be a routine tonsilectomy. The tonsilectomy was performed, and I was sitting beside Linda in a hospital room. The nurse assured me everything was all right. I was reading the newspaper and suddenly I looked at Linda and saw her little head was in a pool of blood. We did not know that she was a free bleeder, but obviously she was. I rushed out of the room into the corridor of the hospital calling for the nurse and the doctor. The nurse came quickly, saw her condition, picked her little body up and ran down the hospital corridor, carrying Linda to emergency surgery. As the nurse disappeared through the double doors on which a sign had been placed which said, "No Admittance," I retreated down the hallway of the hospital to find an empty room where I could pray. I finally saw a room that was dark in which there were no patients. I went to a bedside and knelt and began to pray for God to spare the life of our little girl. The last words I heard the nurse say as she carried Linda down the hallway were, "Call the doctor! She is dying! She is bleeding to death! Call the doctor! Call Dr. Fried-man!" With these words ringing in my mind, I knelt to pray for Linda. Then I said to God, "Before I pray, I want to be sure that You hear me and that You answer me, and I want you to let me know if there is anything between You and me that would hinder my prayers being answered." Suddenly I saw the face of that man in Texas against whom I had ill will. I realized that there was something in my heart that must be removed before Linda could be spared. I rushed out in the hallway, grabbed a telephone to call the man. The operator told me that he had moved. I called a friend of his to find his address and phone number. For a long time in that hallway I frantically tried to find the man so I could apologize, but my efforts failed. I returned to the room to pray. Though I had not accom-plished my mission of apologizing, the Lord had removed bitterness from my heart, and I was sure that He would hear me and answer me. Praise His name, Linda did live, and she is now a wife and mother of two children.

I continued my search for the man. I could not find him. Months later I was preaching in a small church in east Texas. As I walked onto the platform, I looked and to my delight and surprise, that man and his wife were sitting a few seats from me in front of the pulpit. My heart began to beat faster, and I said to God, "If You will let me live through this sermon, I promise You I'll go back and apologize to that man and tell him I love him as soon as the sermon is over." I finished the sermon and during the closing prayer I started back to the man's seat, when suddenly I bumped into somebody. I looked up and it was this deacon. We met in the aisle, and while the closing prayer was still being prayed I looked up and said two words. Now these are the hardest words I say. For many years I have been preaching; in fact, I have preached over 45,000 sermons, and yet there is one little sermon of two words that is the hardest for me to preach. Those two words are the words I knew I had to say to this man, and so with the same awkwardness of a little child making his first speech in school, I looked up through tears and said, "I'm sorry!"

He looked at me and said, "Pastor, I'm sorry! It was my fault that we had the trouble!"

I said, "No, it was my fault."

He said, "No, Pastor, you were tired and weary and I shouldn't have provoked you to say what you said."

"But," I said, "sir, I should not have said what I said and I am sorry!"

He said, "Well, it was my fault," and I said, "No, it was my fault." He said, "It was my fault," and I said, "No, it was my fault." And so we argued for awhile over whose fault it was, as the Lord in Heaven smiled and saw two of His children making it right with each other. That night I went back to my hotel room, took off my shoes and got up on the bed and made a trampoline out of the bed and jumped up and down most of the night and sang, "Nothing between my soul and the Saviour, naught of this world's delusive dreams; I have renounced all sinful pleasure, Jesus is mine—there's nothing between!"

From that moment until this moment I have had many enemies, but I have never been an enemy. I am commanded by God to bless those that curse me, to pray for those that despitefully use me, to do good to those who do evil to me, to love those who hate me.

4. *I am not to attack, nor am I to defend.* A good motto for any Christian would be, "No attack; no defense." By that I mean, I am not to attack my enemies. I am not to return evil for evil. Then, when attacked by my enemies, I make no defense. Now I will defend my Saviour, and I will defend others, but I will not defend myself. I fight His battles; He fights my battles.

5. *I am not to go to court with a Christian brother or sister.* **I Corinthians 6:7, "Now therefore there is utterly a fault among you, because ye go to law one with another. Why do ye not rather take wrong? why do ye not rather suffer yourselves to be defrauded?"**

**Psalm 119:165, "Great peace have they which love Thy law: and nothing shall offend them."**

Our churches and schools are plagued by people who are easily offended. Each of us should constantly be on guard against this deadly enemy of the church, the school, the Christian and the Saviour.

6. *Stay in the Word of God.* **Psalm 119:165** teaches us that there is a way that we can rise above being offended. Notice the words, **"Nothing shall offend them."** Read the Word, memorize the Word, love the Word, meditate upon the Word, live in the Word, and victory can be had over this adversary.

7. *Do not look at criticism as being personal.* Years ago I learned a little exercise that has helped me tremendously. I decided to look upon my critics as broken rather than as bad. When my watch breaks, I do not fight back and throw it against the wall. When my radio breaks, I do not become angry at it. I decided that when people criticize me, it is not because they are bad; it is

because there is a broken part. This does not mean that they should be discarded any more than the radio should be discarded. They need to be fixed. Then I also realize that I too sometimes am broken.

8. *Do not love because of the object.* Love should be caused by the condition of the heart of the lover, not the attributes of the loved. God does not love us because of what we are; He loves us because of what He is. May He help us to be like Him in this respect.

Being human, it may be somewhat difficult for us to love the unlovely as much as we love the lovely, and the degree of our love may be determined by the degree of loveliness; however, the presence of our love should not be so determined.

9. *Do not want things or position.* Most of our hurt feelings are caused by disappointments in not receiving things, acclaim or position that we want or crave. The less one wants the less he will be offended. The more one wants for others, the less he will be offended. The only real want or craving a Christian should have toward others is an intense desire to help others. Remember, Christ has no alternative but to love the unlovely, the unloving and often the unloved.

10. *If your critic is your inferior, allow that he has not been privileged to know what you know.* Give him some leeway.

I am a very criticized man, probably one of the most criticized preachers of this generation. I try to allow that a person can dislike me and still not be bad. We are so constructed that a person can be mean to the rest of the world and good to us and we think he is good, or he can be good to the rest of the world and mean to us and we think he is bad. There are many people who have not had the teachings that you and I have had. They do not even know the truths that we are now sharing. No one criticizes a baby because he cannot ride a bicycle or a child because he doesn't know trigonometry. Why should we have our feelings hurt by those who have not been privileged to learn not to be critical?

11. *Do not have a lot of unplanned fellowship.* Do not just sit around and talk. Soon it will lead to talking about people. Someone

has said that great minds talk about ideas, good minds talk about things, and weak minds talk about people. When planning to get together with other Christians, plan the activities. Do not sit idly and talk idly. There is a grave temptation to talk too much about people. Maybe this talk is not bad, but once we idly talk, we are tempted to talk about people, and once we start talking about people, we are tempted to say bad things about them.

12. *Do not retaliate to those who try to offend you, who are unkind to you or who criticize you.*

Memorize **Psalm 119:165.** Believe it. Practice it and let nothing offend you.

Would you rather for two people to hurt or one? Of course, the answer is that all of us would rather one person hurt than two.

Would it matter who these two people were? Why initially we would answer the question, "No, it doesn't matter who they are. I would rather for only one person to hurt than two."

The next question comes—what if one of those two people is you? Then, will it matter? In other words, would you rather only one to hurt or two to hurt if you are the one that is hurt, or would you rather someone else hurt because you hurt?

Now ask yourself this next question—would it matter how the other person felt about you? In other words, if you are hurting because another person has hurt you and that other person hates you, would you still rather one person to hurt than two? When our answer to this question can become "Yes," then we are approaching what Christianity is all about and the type of life that God's people are supposed to live. Probably the PhD of Christianity is earned when a person can treat his enemies as Jesus treated His. Perhaps the most difficult and last step of Christian maturity is when the Christian learns to love those who hate him, pray for those who despitefully use him, bless those who curse him and do good to those who do evil to him.

Someone very dear to me who had been my friend for years launched a brief but fierce attack my way. I could not believe he did it. When I realized he did, I could not believe he meant to do me harm. Through tears I wrote these words:

## Let's Both Forgive!

You did not mean to loose the bow
That launched the arrow toward my breast;
Nor did you plan to shake the limb
That so disturbed my downy nest.

'Twas not your will to hurl the stones
That hailed upon me like a storm;
'Twas not your quill that penned the darts
That railed upon my inner form.

You did not make the venom that
Your tongue so quickly shot my way;
Nor did you mean to loosen all
The fiery snakes I fled today.

You did not weigh the giant stone
Hewn by the words you spoke to me.
'Twould not be there had you but known
The load with which I came to thee.

I know, for I have hurled some stones,
I vainly tried to have returned.
My quiver's empty far too oft;
My fiery darts too much have burned.

I own some venom and a bow
Which oft unite in deadly flight
To far exceed in damage done
The arrow's wound and serpent's bite.

I know the empty victor's guilt
When kneeling o'er my fallen prey.
I've held the sword when blood was spilt,
While joys of winning fled away.

So may I love you when you hate,
And may I bless you when you curse.
I cannot now retaliate,
For yesterday 'twas in reverse.

May I return an answer soft
To turn away thy hasty wrath;
For I have tasted far too oft
The bitter herb my friend now hath.


Six critical letters came in one day's mail—five of the letters criticizing someone else! I find myself having a difficult time believing that God's people can be so critical of each other. Spontaneously I shouted while alone in my study, "Could we not love each other?" I then used the following words to plead with fellow Christians to love our brothers and sisters in Christ:

### Could We Not Love Each Other?

Could we not love each other?
The place prepared for me
Is near the one for thee.
Hence, neighbors we will be.
Come! Be my brother.

Could we not love each other?
The Hand that gives thee bread
Is the One that keeps me fed.
Let harsh words be unsaid.
You are my brother.

Could we not love each other?
The load your heart doth bear
Is one that we could share.
We both dwell 'neath His care,
Beloved brother.

Could we not love each other?
I have stood in your place,
And you my path oft traced,
So let us offer grace
Befitting brothers.

Could we not love each other?
The One Who died for you
Is my dear Saviour too.
Is it too much to do
To love our brother?

Could we not love each other?
That selfsame throne of grace
Where thou dost seek His face
Is my abiding place
Beside you, brother.

Could we not love each other?

The letter was filled with hatred, insults and satire. It was from one who admitted hatred for me. I called him on the telephone to seek conciliation. This attempt simply turned written words to spoken ones. All efforts for a Christian understanding failed and he hung up the phone. I wrote the following words and mailed them to him.

### You Are My Enemy

You are my enemy—
So I must love you more
Than those who love me most,
And, who, upon me pour
The best of friendship's wine.
I must not taste the sour grape
From vindication's vine.

You are my enemy—
'Twill not be always so;
For I will drown thy hate
Within the loving flow
Of calm, forgiving seas;
And use thy saber's sharpest blows
To knock me to my knees.

You are my enemy—
I must take care to bless
Thee through thy cursings oft!
And hold within my breast
That restless, unkind word;
For I must keep in hidden sheath
Retaliation's sword.

You are my enemy—
I cannot quench the scorn
That you have rushed my way;
Yet something hath been born,
Begotten from above;
No shield you hold can deftly block
The arrows of my love.

You are my enemy—
And so I more must pray
For God to do thee good,
And take my spite away;
And warm the biting chill
That cometh to the both of us
Should I but do thee ill.

One day, upon hearing of an attack on me and my ministry, I was tempted to retaliate and to steal from the Lord His work of vengeance. I began to think, however, of the times when I had been critical and unkind. Hence, I could not retaliate. Rather than give vengeance, I must offer compassion, love, and understanding. The following stanzas came to my mind:

### A Familiar Stone

I once retrieved an angry stone,
Still warm from resting in thine hand,
To boomerang it back to thee,
As vengeful reprimand.

I took retaliatory aim
To even up the score;
Then saw the rock I grimly held,
Was one I'd seen before.

Oh, my! It had my fingerprint!
Beloved, could it be . . .
That this same stone that came my way,
Was one I hurled at thee?

Hence, I'll not aim its point thy way,
Nor hurl it back to thee;
I'll bury it and ask our God
To forgive both thee and me.

# Chapter 11

# Treatment of Those
# Who Are Stumblingblocks

**Matthew 18:7, "Woe unto the world because of offences! for it must needs be that offences come; but woe to that man by whom the offence cometh!"** Notice the word "offence." Simply stated, an offence is a stumblingblock. It is the leading or attempting to lead another to do wrong, or to prevent another from doing right. This may be done purposely or it may be a stumblingblock that is dropped by negligence or carelessness. In any case, our Lord plainly teaches that to leave stumblingblocks is a fault. In some cases, it may be a grievous fault; in other cases, a slight one. Nevertheless, it is wrong to lead another into sin or to prevent another from doing good. These are called stumblingblocks.

These obstacles to good are found in every church in America and every organization of every church. They are found on Sunday school faculties, on Christian school faculties, on deacon boards, in Christian school classrooms, church choirs, church staffs and even in Christian colleges. Those who place purposely or carelessly drop these stumblingblocks will attempt to lead the Christian into wrong by offering them everything from a joint of marijuana to a juicy bit of gossip. Let us notice how they operate.

1. *They will lead you to do wrong when they know it is wrong.* This is the worst form of stumblingblocks. There are those who know something is wrong, who will attempt to lead you to do that wrong. It is done most commonly by those who are doing wrong

themselves and do not want to be alone in their wrongdoing. The tragedy of it all is that it is often done in the name of friendship, which God meant to be one of the greatest blessings of the Christian life. What a tragedy when such a great blessing is perverted into a curse!

Sometimes the tempter will even demand the price of losing his friendship if temptation is rejected and resisted. He is leading you to believe that you may purchase his friendship at this ridiculously high price! If this were possible, such is far from being worth the purchase! A so-called friend who wishes his so-called friend to do wrong in order to keep his friendship is no friend at all! When you attempt to purchase friendship, it is always counterfeit. This tempting may be done by someone who is addicted to narcotics attempting to ensnare another in his habit. It may be done by a young person demanding proof of the love of a member of the opposite sex by insisting that person join him in immorality. It may be done by one who is disloyal to leadership attempting to lead another to share his disloyalty.

Nearly every week I receive phone calls from pastors having internal problems in their churches. The story is always the same; it never varies. When a pastor tells me he is having trouble in his church, I can write the script. For that matter, the script is already written. Some man of prominence in the church is attempting to hurt the pastor, his ministry and his leadership. He is not satisfied with his own sin; he wants others to join him and so he places stumblingblocks in the path of the loyalty of others. Many sincere people have stumbled over these blocks and have been caused much grief in days to come.

This behavior is as old as mankind. Moses and Aaron faced the same thing that the sincere pastors face today. **Numbers 16:1-3, "Now Korah, the son of Izhar, the son of Kohath, the son of Levi, and Dathan and Abiram, the sons of Eliab, and On, the son of Peleth, sons of Reuben, took men: and they rose up before Moses, with certain of the children of Israel, two hundred and fifty princes of the assembly, famous in the congrega-**

**tion, men of renown: and they gathered themselves together against Moses and against Aaron, and said unto them, Ye take too much upon you, seeing all the congregation are holy, every one of them, and the Lord is among them: wherefore then lift ye up yourselves above the congregation of the Lord?"**

Notice in **verse 2, "And they rose up before Moses."** Notice in **verse 3, "And they gathered themselves together against Moses and against Aaron."**

Now notice in **verse 2** who they were. Look at the words, **"two hundred and fifty princes of the assembly, famous in the congregation, men of renown."** The Devil hasn't changed his methods, has he? The same thing happens today as it did over three millenniums ago.

Now notice their charges in **verse 3, "Ye take too much upon you, seeing all the congregation are holy."** Notice later on in **verse 3, "Wherefore then lift ye up yourselves above the congregation of the Lord?"** Everything that goes around comes around, and Satan is not very original. His methods are the same from generation to generation.

2. *They will lead you to do what they do not think is wrong but what you think is wrong.* They want to convince you that you should go against your conscientious convictions, and they want to persuade you to disobey your scruples. "Nothing is wrong with that!" is never spoken by a true friend. A true friend will allow you to have your own convictions and will want you to abide by them and live by them. He will respect your convictions and not attempt to lower yours to his.

3. *They will lead you not to do right.* It is wrong if we make Christian duty and the Christian life difficult to our fellow-Christians when we should do our best to make it easy. We have tremendous power over each other. Our personalities, our conversation and our habits are almost sure in some degree either to help or hinder each other. One may encourage and tempt another to do wrong by good-natured behavior when his friend is doing wrong, or he may prove his friendship by being disagreeable when

his friend is about to do wrong. What I am saying is that we may try to help a friend in such a way as to provoke him or perplex him, so we are not only to refrain from leading another to doing wrong, but we should actively encourage him to do right.

How then should the one be treated who becomes a stumblingblock and who places stumblingblocks in our path of righteousness?

1. *Do not become a stumblingblock to him by stumbling over his stumblingblock.* The tempter sins against the tempted, but when the tempted yields, he likewise sins against the tempter. He has placed a crown of evil on the other man's sin of being the tempter. He has completed the job attempted by the tempter, and just as the one who is tempting him has aided in his sin, his committing the sin has also added to the sin of the one who tempted him.

If we refuse to stumble over the stumblingblock, we save the one who placed it there from committing an even greater evil and, for that matter, another evil. The tempter cannot become the accomplice to a crime that has not been committed, so in a sense when we yield to his temptation, we sin against him, even as he sinned against us. The tempter sins when placing the stumblingblock in the path of the tempted. The tempted sins when he stumbles. He also causes the tempter to sin twofold because the tempter's sin is now completed and doubled.

Let us illustrate. A man who is drinking offers another a drink. He has sinned in so doing because he has placed a stumblingblock in the path of righteousness of the one who is offered the drink. When the one who is tempted takes the drink, he sins; but he has also sinned against the one who offered him the drink, who sinned in drinking, who sinned in tempting his neighbor to drink, and has now become an accomplice in his neighbor's sin of drink. He now is guilty of three sins instead of two.

A young man tries to seduce a young woman into immorality. He sins in so doing, but the young woman who yields has completed his sin and the seducer's sin is now twofold.

2. *Refuse immediately.* **Psalm 119:60, "I made haste, and**

**delayed not to keep Thy commandments."** The easiest time to refuse evil is NOW. It is often very hard not only to do what is right, but to do it at the time that right should be done. This Psalm not only exalts the doing of right but the doing of right immediately. Every Christian is bound not only to be obedient to the call of duty but to be instantly obedient to that call. There is a tremendous difference between the beauty of obedience, which has the spontaneity of a little child running to do something for Mother who finds a delightful pleasure in the sense of obedience, and that obedience which comes unwillingly and which is done slowly as if it is no more than an absolute MUST.

In practically every case of obedience, delay makes it more difficult. Nothing can be gained by cautious procrastinating obedience. That obedience does not become easier but harder. There is no obedience as delightful as ready obedience. It brings a charm with it. It prevents many temptations by simply giving them no time to do their work. It conquers many difficulties by its own impulse, and it leaves us with a warm awareness that we belong to God and we are wanting to please Him. It also saves us oftentimes from committing sin because as has been stated, the easiest time to refuse is NOW!

When such instant refusal is performed enough times, it will become instinctive. It will become a part of the subconscious and hence, becomes character. Character is the subconscious doing of right. It is the doing of right by reflex. It is resisting temptation by instinct.

3. *Do not travel with those who carry stumblingblocks.* In every church and church organization, there are such people. It is not difficult for us to know who they are. If we are wise, we will be nice to them, courteous to them and gracious to them, but we will not travel with them.

There is a divided four-lane interstate highway leading from the Hammond area to Indianapolis, Indiana. It is Interstate 65. This highway goes through no towns, has few if any stops and is, of course, divided four-lane all the way. Then there is the old highway that leads to Indianapolis. It is Highway 41. Leaving the Hammond area on Highway 41, one must go through Highland, Indiana, where there are at least five or six stoplights; Schererville, Indiana, where there are two more stoplights. He must then go through St. John, Indiana; Cedar Lake, Indiana; and other small towns and cities along the way. The person who wants to take the fastest and safest trip to Indianapolis will certainly choose Interstate 65. He will not condemn Highway 41, criticize Highway 41 or gossip about Highway 41; he will simply forget Highway 41. Highway 41 will not be a part of his thinking processes as he journeys to Indianapolis; he simply takes the road without the stumblingblocks. The wise Christian will do the same thing. He will take the road not traveled by the one who lays stumblingblocks in his way. He will not criticize him or attempt to hurt him; he will simply not be aware that he exists. He is too busy traveling with those who want to help him in righteousness and not be his accomplice in sin!

# Chapter 12

# Why We Have Strife in Our Churches

Why do Christian people (or for that matter, any people) have strife between themselves? The answer plainly and simply is, "unfulfilled appetites." We had a desire or appetite to receive something which we did not receive. We had a desire or an appetite to be treated in a certain way, and the desired treatment never came. In other words, we did not get the thing or the treatment that we wanted. Of course, the secret to avoiding the strife caused by these unfulfilled appetites is to have sanctified appetites and to keep our wants and desires within the limits of our ability to have.

A good definition of riches would be as follows: "the balancing of wants and possessions." So, there are two ways to be rich. One is being able to afford what one wants, and the other is wanting only what one can afford. The secret is the balancing of the wants and the possessions. I am rich if I can get what I want. I am rich if I want what I have.

Most of us will never be able to get what an unrestrained appetite would want us to have, but all of us can balance the equation and become rich by asking God to sanctify our appetites and our wants. **Psalm 37:4, "Delight thyself also in the Lord; and He shall give thee the desires of thine heart."** The average casual reader of the Bible could misunderstand this passage. We could mistakenly think that God is telling us that if we want a Rolls Royce car, we can have it; if we want a half-million dollar house, we can have it; if we want a $25,000 diamond ring, we can have it. This application is totally contrary to the teaching of the Scripture. In the first place, if we delight ourselves in the Lord, our desires can be sanctified and we can grow to want what we have. God is not saying here that He will increase what we have to fulfill the lust of the carnal nature. He is saying that if we delight ourselves in Him, our desires will become equal with our possessions.

Some interpret the Scripture to mean that if we delight ourselves in the Lord, He will give us what we want. I rather prefer to believe that God is saying if we delight ourselves in the Lord, He will give us what TO want, and when He is saying He will give us our desires, I feel that He is saying that He will give us our appetites as well as the fulfillment of our appetites. It may be in that some cases He will increase our possessions to equal our desires. It may be that other cases He will lower our desires to equal our possessions. Whichever it is, it is simply the balancing of the equation, which in the end makes one rich, for he has what he wants and wants what he has.

This is the same thing that God is telling us in **John 15:7, "If ye abide in Me, and My words abide in you, ye shall ask what ye will, and it shall be done unto you."** We emphasize the part of that verse which tells us to ask what we want and we can get it. God is emphasizing the part that says, **"If ye abide in Me, and My words abide in you."** The word "abide" implies "to live." If we live in and for and through Christ and His Word lives in and through us, our appetites become sanctified and God can give us carte blanche and power of attorney to ask what we will because He trusts what we WILL ask. We cannot be so trusted unless we abide in Him and His words abide in us.

**Romans 8:28** would certainly shed some light on this truth: **"And we know that all things work together for good to them that love God, to them who are the called according to His purpose."** Once again God is reminding us that spiritual people may feel free to ask what they want because God can trust their wants. We like to think that if we love God and are in His will, everything will work out for our good, and this certainly is true. However, what we think of as being good changes when we love God and are living in His will. The very same thing that was going to happen to us becomes for our good if we love Him and if we are in His will.

Let's suppose that a Christian is not living in the will of God and is not filled with love for Christ. The events that come his way do not work for his good. However, take those same events and put them in his path under different conditions, those conditions being that he now loves God and is in the will of God, and they will work for his good. Once again, the difference is in the appetite. When a person delights himself in the Lord as in **Psalm 37:4**, and abides in Christ and God's words abide in him, and he loves God and lives in the will of God, he then has sanctified appetites that make it possible for his desires and possessions to be equal, which is in the final analysis the definition of riches.

The wise Christian will not allow himself to possess appetites that cannot be filled. It is a blessed truth that if he meets the conditions of the aforementioned Scriptures, his appetites will be inside the will of God; and any appetite that is inside the will of God will be filled by God, for He promises to give us the desires of our hearts if those desires have been purified and sanctified.

This leads us to another thought, and that is, WE WANT WHAT WE GIVE.

1. *We want the same type love that we give.* Even our Lord came to Peter and asked, "Lovest thou Me?" The word here for love is the word that is used for God's love. It is a deep, abiding love. Peter answered, "Thou knowest that I love Thee," but Peter's word for love was the love that we would call something like fondness. Jesus was saying, "Peter, do you deeply love Me?" and Peter was saying, "Lord, Thou knowest that I am fond of Thee." Jesus, in using the word for deep love, was actually saying, "Peter, do you love Me like I love you?" Jesus can make such a request because His love is perfect, but for us to want to be loved like we love can create an unfulfilled appetite. Our appetite should be to love deeply rather than to be loved deeply.

Years ago when our son, David, was Youth Director at First Baptist Church, an interesting thing happened. It was comencement night for Hammond Baptist High School. After commencement had ended, I had an appointment with one of our ladies. While I was counseling with her, there was a knock on my door. I went to the door and David was at the door crying uncontrollably and asking for me to speak with him for a few moments. I told him that I had an appointment, and he said, "Dad, I've got to see you right now! It's an emergency! It can't wait!"

I asked the little lady with whom I was counseling if she would wait, and I stepped across the hallway into my secretary's office so Dave and I could be alone. I said, "What's the trouble, Doc?"

He said, "Dad, it just dawned on me that those young people that just graduated are no longer in our youth department. I have lost them!" (I think this was the first group that David had lost since being Youth Director.) "I love them, Dad! It just dawned on me that I don't have them any more, and Dad, I just had to get with somebody who could love me like I love them. That's why, Dad, I had to be with you."

I said, "You found him, Doc," and I hugged him and we shared some tender moments together.

Now the truth is that Dave's appetite was filled, but suppose that he had had that appetite hundreds of miles from his dad. He would have had a tough evening, because there would have been no fulfillment of his appetite.

The wise Christian will let his appetite be to love. That can always be fulfilled because it is within the grasp of his will. Don't misunderstand this. I am not saying that we should not want to be loved, but I am saying we should not want to be loved exactly like we love, because no one loves exactly alike, which is why God made us all different. Each of us has a unique way of loving Christ that no one else has, and since each love, though given by God and with God as its source, is different, it is impossible for us to be loved exactly like we love. So, if someone doesn't love us like we want to be loved, and if we want to be loved like we love, it is easy to be upset.

There are few things that hurt as much as wanting to be loved like we love and not being loved that way. This hurt is increased the more deeply one loves, because the more refined one's love is, the harder it is to find reciprocation. This also makes it easier to be lonely. What I am saying is that the Christian should find the presence of his joy in loving, and then perhaps he can find the degree of that joy in being loved. In other words, I have joy simply because I love you. Now if you return that love, it increases my joy, but if you do not, my joy is still present.

So whether it be possessions or treatment, there is an atmosphere conducive to strife if I want something and do not receive it. You did not treat me the way I wanted you to treat me. You did not say what I wanted you to say. You did not do what I wanted you to do. You did not give me what I wanted you to give me. You did not express to me what I wanted you to express to me. In other words, you did not fulfill my appetites.

2. *We want the same type expressions of love that we give.* There are certain ways that each of us says, "I love you," and most of us want love to be expressed the same way we express love. We want to get what we give. For example, men and women do not express love the same way. Many marriages have to endure strife because the husband wants the wife to love him the same way that he loves her and to express it the same way. Now to be sure, the wise wife will try to find the expressions of her love that her husband would desire, but the basic fact is that men and women do not express their love to each other in the same way. The man may just want a quick hug and kiss. The woman may want soft music and atmosphere. The man calls the woman unaffectionate, and the woman calls the man unromantic. This is because the appetites have conformed to each one's own expressions of love. A certain expression of love is wanted and though the love may be expressed, since it is not what was wanted, it often causes strife.

In a sense, this is almost what could be called mental homosexuality. For example, a man may want a woman's love, but he may want it to be mentally the same love that he gives her. In other words, he wants her to love him emotionally and mentally like a man, but she is not a man! She is a woman, and she must love him emotionally and mentally as a woman would love him. So, instead of wanting his love returned, it is much better for him simply to want whatever type love that God has given her for him to be expressed in her own way, not in his!

This same thing could be true between the young and the old. This is one reason that teenagers and adults have a difficult time understanding each other. The parent kisses the teenager. The teenager seems indifferent, which causes the parent to be displeased and causes strife. The wise parent will let the teenager love like the teenager loves. Teenagers cannot return adult love to adults. They can only give teenage love. The wise parent will accept it with rejoicing and gratitude in whatever manner of expression the teenager uses.

3. *We want the same type logic that we give.* We want others to logic like we logic, and an appetite is created for us to receive that kind of logic. Since all people do not logic alike, that appetite is often unsatisfied, and strife is a result! A man may want a woman to logic like he does, while a woman may want a man to logic like she does. An adult may want a teenager to logic as an adult, and the teenager may want the adult to logic like a teenager. When such appetites are created or allowed to exist, they are often unfulfilled and cause strife. In other words, I want you to see things exactly as I see them. When you do not see things exactly as I see them, my appetite is unfulfilled!

Recently I was preaching in another state. I told the people that I would appreciate it if they would help me to be heard by helping to prevent any unnecessary interruptions in the service. I was to be there for only two nights, and certainly I would not want, for example, a crying baby to limit the effectiveness of my message. I wanted to help the people! After I had preached a few minutes, a baby began to cry (at least I thought it was a baby) in the back of the auditorium. The people in that section were disturbed and unable to follow the message. I stopped the service and asked whoever had the baby to take it to the nursery. Someone got up and left, and I thought that they had granted my request. The disturbance was stopped and we had a wonderful service. After the service, a lady came to talk to me who was very disturbed! She told me that she was the one who had the child who misbehaved, but that the child was not a baby! The "child" was an afflicted teenager, and the lady was very disturbed that I had asked her to remove her daughter. I went out to the car where the daughter and the rest of the family were waiting for the lady, and I saw the child. It was a tragic thing! Though she was in her late teen years, her little body was deformed, and it was a heartbreak to see.

It was obvious that the lady was wanting me to apologize for asking her to take the child out of the service when she was causing a disturbance. I certainly expressed my compassion, my sympathy and my love, but I could not tell her that I would not do the same thing again. As a preacher, I had a message to deliver! It was to me the most important thing in the world! As a mother, she had a child that she felt had been mistreated, and that was the most important thing to her! It would have been totally impossible for us to logic the same way. Because of that, I was not offended in the least. I had no appetite for her to logic as I did. Because of that, I had nothing but love toward her. On the other hand, the dear lady wanted me to logic as she did. She had an appetite for me to do so, and it was impossible for me to satisfy this appetite. Of course, her family shared her feelings, and they had ill will toward me. The reason for this ill will was that they had a desire for me to logic as they did. I had no ill will toward them because I did not have a desire for them to see it my way. I didn't blame them at all for seeing it their way. Consequently, she had a want that could not be balanced with a possession. I had no such want.

Now let us suppose for a moment that I had the same appetite that she had had. Suppose that I just could not understand it because she couldn't see it my way. Why couldn't she understand that a preacher's message is so important! Why couldn't she understand because that I had traveled 700 miles to bring two messages, I certainly wanted to be heard and must be heard! Why couldn't she understand that I was not being selfish in the matter! I was wanting to help people, and there were hundreds of people there who needed to be helped, and the disturbance caused by her child was preventing them from receiving that help!

If I had insisted in my own mind that our logic be reconciled, I would have been as disturbed with her as she was with me. This is where strife originates. "Why can't you see it my way?" "I just don't understand you." "You're not making sense." These are statements that represent the cause of strife. I think the way we put it usually is that we just don't see it eye to eye. If we don't see eye to eye, and if both of us insist that we see eye to eye, there is strife. On the other hand, if both of us could express our opinions, not desiring a reconciling of logic, we can disagree and not have strife.

This is what causes strife in our churches. Far too many of us have appetites that warrant certain treatment. When that treatment does not come, there is strife. The same thing causes strife at home, at work and at play. On the other hand, if our appetite is to love others, to express that love to others, and to help others, then that appetite can be fulfilled.

Do not want to be treated in a certain way; rather, want to treat the other person properly. Do not want expressions of gratitude; rather, want to expess gratitude. Do not want folks to appreciate you; just want to appreciate them. Most of our problems in our churches would be solved if our desires, wants and appetites were purified and sanctified!

# Chapter 13

# Act—Don't React!

In an athletic contest the offense always has the advantage because the offense knows the play. They determine the action. The defense reacts to the action of the offense, which places them at a severe handicap. For example, in football a wide receiver runs down the field to catch a pass. He knows whether he is going to stop abruptly, cut to the right, cut to the left or run full-speed ahead. He knows where the ball is to be thrown and where he is to be when the ball is thrown. The defensive man has no idea. He simply has to react to the actions of the offensive player.

The Christian should stay on the offense! Reaction means that someone else is determining your behavior. Only you can destroy yourself. No one else can destroy you unless you allow him to do so. The only thing that can destroy a peron is self-destruction, and self-destruction is caused by improper reaction. Consequently, one can be destroyed by another only when the actions of the enemy cause an improper reaction.

One of the interesting and sad things about improper reaction is that we react to our reaction. In other words, if someone provokes another to improper reaction, he then reacts to his own reaction and digs a deeper hole. Reaction takes a person away from the control of his own destiny. There are several things that should be considered concerning action and reaction.

1. *Do not spend casual time with people who entice you to react*

*wrongly.* There are people whose behavior causes an unwise reaction. They may "rub you the wrong way." Find out who these people are and don't let them rub you. There are some people whose actions may cause one to react with quick temper. There are people whose actions would cause one to react with slothfulness. There are people whose actions would cause one to react with yielding to temptation. There are people whose actions would cause one to react with bitterness. Be nice to these people. Work with them if you must, but do not spend casual time with them. Everything should be planned when you are together so as not to give the person a chance to exhibit his behavior or actions that would cause an unwise reaction on your part.

2. *Do not read materials that make you react unwisely.* I grew up in Dallas, Texas. Because of that I grew up following the Dallas sports teams. This has made me a rabid Dallas Cowboy fan, a Dallas Maverick fan and a fan of nearly all the sports teams in and around Dallas. Then, too, I am interested in the news of my hometown. Because of this, for years I have taken a Dallas newspaper. At first I subscribed to one of the two newspapers, but there is a sports writer in one of those papers who has a terrible habit of unnecessary and extreme criticism of the local sports teams. He is so cynical that just to read his column stirs me to anger and almost contempt. One day I reminded myself that I did not have to subscribe to that newspaper, so I changed my subscription to the other Dallas paper. This was done because I did not want to read that which made me react unwisely. The same would apply to radio talk shows, television talk shows, television preachers, etc. There are some talk shows that I know will provoke me to anger and disgust and will cause me to react unwisely. Since I do not want my behavior controlled by liberals, humanists, modernists and critics, I do not listen to them, read their articles or subscribe to their publications.

I know many preachers whose preaching is simply that of reaction. They read things all week that make them mad, and then they preach on Sunday against those things. This makes for interesting preaching and will keep a good crowd coming for a little while, but it is preaching that is simply reacting to improper stimuli and will not build great Christians. Do not misunderstand me. I believe in preaching against sin, but one is supposed to hate sin, not because an undesirable creature is for it; he is supposed to hate sin because it is contrary to the will of God and the good of man. The right kind of a preacher will not need the enemy to provoke him to anger. He can provoke himself to anger by the realization of the awfulness of the sin. Much of our preaching against sin is not preaching against sin; it is preaching against sinners!

The wise Christian will not allow himself to be exposed to those things that take his initiative away and enable his behavior to simply be a series of reactions to someone else who has turned him on by their actions.

3. *Be oblivious to what makes you react unwisely.* I travel every week. I preach hundreds of sermons a year all over America. (In fact, this chapter is being dictated as I drive down the side of a mountain in the northwest part of our country.) I sometimes have to sit through music that could cause me to react. When such is the case, I become oblivious to that music, and during the song service and during the special music I discipline my mind to be on something else—usually on the message I am to preach and the truth I am to present. Occasionally a preacher who speaks before me will say things contrary to the truth. The temptation is for me to leave what God has given me for the congregation and to start chasing that preacher. In so doing, I get to blow off some steam and get to tell the preacher and the people what I thought about the first sermon, and the people go without what God had given me for them! Normally I simply think of the great truth that I am going to present and become oblivious to the first preacher.

On two occasions in my ministry after I preached a sermon, the pastor of the church where I preached stood to tell the people that he did not agree with my sermon and he took several minutes expressing points of disagreement and reasons for the disagreement! In one instance I had to preach again within 15 minutes. The other time I had to preach again that evening. Of course, the natural tendency is for me to make my rebuttal in the next message, but the natural tendency is not usually right, so in both cases I proceeded to preach the message that I was going to preach without making a rebuttal at all. Why should I cause the people to suffer because I had been injured! Why should I preach a reactionary sermon when I had already decided the course of action that I felt the Holy Spirit wanted me to follow!

4. *Plan your reactions.* By that I mean, foresee battles that may arise and times when you will be compelled by conviction and circumstances to respond to someone else's behavior. Take some time. Sit down for awhile. Think of possible actions that you may have to follow and to which you may have to respond. Decide beforehand what you are going to say and do. Do not let the spur of the moment cause you to react unwisely but in the prayerful quiet of your own study or room, decide yourself what your reaction will be to certain forms of behavior. This changes your reaction to action, since you have decided what you are going to do before the other person has done it. This enables you to have more time to decide. It enables you to decide before the heat of the battle, and it enables you to decide without emotion.

Twenty-eight years ago I became Pastor of the First Baptist Church of Hammond. The first year was a hectic one. People set themselves against my ministry and made serious attempts to force my resignation. A special night was set when we would thrash out the problems and the people would be allowed to ask me questions from the floor. For hours I sat in the basement of our parsonage and tried to predict what questions would be asked. I came to the conclusion that each question that would be asked me would be one of seventeen. I wrote these seventeen questions and made a full-page outline as to how I would answer each question when and if it were asked. Though all the questions were not asked at this special meeting, there were no questions asked that were not on my list. Consequently, when each question was asked, I did not have to react, for I had planned my reaction beforehand, making it an action. So when the question was asked, I simply pulled out the prepared answer and read it. This was done calmly without emotion and not in a reactionary spirit. This probably saved the First Baptist Church of Hammond for the cause of fundamentalism and probably for the cause of usefulness. Any time one expects behavior that would tempt to improper reaction, he would be wise to plan his reactions to that behavior, making his reactions not reactions at all but actions because they were planned before the behavior was planned.

(1) *Plan your reaction to criticism.* The flesh hates to be criticized, and when criticism comes, it is often prompt in retaliating with unwise reaction. The wise Christian will have a course of action already planned that he may follow when criticism arises.

(2) *Plan your reaction to things that anger you.* Each of us knows things that more readily provoke him. When such actions occur, the temptation is greater to react unwisely. The wise Christian will list these provocative things and will prepare in advance his reaction to them.

(3) *Plan the things for which you would fight.* No one should fight impulsively. Consequently, the person with character will plan the things for which he would fight and will plan the manner of the fight. He will not fight in response to temporary provocation; he will fight only for those things that are predetermined and in a manner that is predetermined.

I have a list of things written down and placed in a drawer in my office for which I would fight. I have a list of things for which I would die. Consequently, I will not fight or die in a quick response to an impulse. My fighting, even unto the death, will be predetermined in the prayerful quiet of my office.

Someone perhaps would say, "I just don't believe in turning it on and off like that." Nor do I believe that. I find it impossible to turn it on and off, but I find it possible to turn on what turns it on and turn off what turns it off. In other words, I can control what controls me and not allow myself to be controlled by the passion of an immediate response to a stimulus that causes me to react unwisely.

I do this concerning the church services. I prayerfully decide in the quiet of my study what my reaction would be when a baby begins to cry in the service. I likewise decide what my action would be if baby continues to cry in the service. I have planned action that I carry out when I am disturbed briefly in a service and other planned action for disturbances I know will not end without my help. This prevents me from acting impulsively and doing something for which I will be sorry later. The people in the audience may or may not agree with my response to the disturbance, but I will have done what I think is best because it is what I thought was best in the quiet of my study before the disturbance arose.

5. *Learn to whom you can trust your reactions.* There are some people with whom you can feel perfectly comfortable and whom you can completely trust not to lead you to unwise reaction. Know these people. They are usually people who think, philosophize and would rather speak of ideas than of people. Someone has said, "Great minds speak about ideas; good minds speak about things; weak minds speak about people."

I am thinking now of a dear friend, Pastor Bruce Porter, in Islamorada, Florida. For many years I have preached for him. I have learned that I can trust my reactions to him. He will not provoke me to unwise reactions. He wants to learn. He wants to talk about ideas that are constructive. He does not indulge in people-talk, so I feel perfectly at ease to have a casual conversation with him. In fact, I enjoy doing so. He meets me at the airport when I make my annual visit to his church. I do not make plans concerning our conversation. I do not need to, for I know he will provoke me to good thoughts and not to unwise reactions.

On the contrary, there are other people to whom I cannot trust my reactions. I would find myself on the defensive. I would find myself not wanting to talk about other people, and I have learned that their conversation would tempt me to reactions that would be unwise and perhaps even divisive.

The wise person will discover such people in order to find out to whom he can and cannot trust his reactions. In the case of the latter, you might want to plan the conversation and think of some questions that you could ask him in order that you may control the conversation, making it necessary for him to react to your behavior rather than your reacting to his behavior.

6. *Spread the word that you do not participate in criticism.* Let it be known that you are not interested in character assassinations nor personality critiques. Word will soon get around, and you will have the reputation for not being critical. People will either respect what they know is your desire or they will be fearful of approaching you with negative subjects.

For years I have traveled the length and breadth of this nation. It is understood all across America that there are certain subjects about which I do not speak. My reputation precedes me, which makes it much easier for me to avoid situations that would be tempting to unwise reaction.

7. *Do not live in unplanned situations.* Idle time is one of the great causes for unnecessary and unwise reaction. Just sitting around and talking with nothing planned leads to differences, arguments, fusses and reactionary conversation.

One of the great problems of our society is that it is built on critique. It is falsely assumed by many that the ability to critique someone is a sign of strength. Nothing could be farther from the truth! To attack the strong is not a sign of strength. To do nothing but critique those who do something is certainly not a sign of strength. The time was, for example, when the local sports writer was a cheerleader for the local team. He has now become the Devil's advocate and is considered somewhat of a successful sports writer if he can criticize the coach. Men who have never carried a football, thrown a pass, kicked a field goal or made a tackle seem to know more about coaching than men who have coached for a lifetime. The pew critiques the pulpit. The student critiques the teacher, and the press critiques everybody! One can hardly listen to a radio station without finding movie critics, restaurant critics and a bevy of other self-styled experts whose only talent is criticizing talent, whose only strength is criticizing strength, whose only accomplishment is shooting at those who have accomplished.

God, give us men who act, not men who react! Give us men with the character to determine their behavior and who decide their own course of action!

# Chapter 14

# Leaders and Followers

Ephesians 5:21-29, "Submitting yourselves one to another in the fear of God. Wives, submit yourselves unto your own husbands, as unto the Lord. For the husband is the head of the wife, even as Christ is the head of the church: and He is the saviour of the body. Therefore as the church is subject unto Christ, so let the wives be to their own husbands in every thing. Husbands, love your wives, even as Christ also loved the church, and gave Himself for it; that He might sanctify and cleanse it with the washing of water by the Word, that He might present it to Himself a glorious church, not having spot, or wrinkle, or any such thing; but that it should be holy and without blemish. So ought men to love their wives as their own bodies. He that loveth his wife loveth himself. For no man ever yet hated his own flesh; but nourisheth and cherisheth it, even as the Lord the church."

Ephesians 6:1, 4, 5, "Children, obey your parents in the Lord: for this is right. And, ye fathers, provoke not your children to wrath: but bring them up in the nurture and admonition of the Lord. Servants, be obedient to them that are your masters according to the flesh, with fear and trembling, in singleness of your heart, as unto Christ."

Ephesians 5:21 is a startling verse, "Submitting yourselves one to another in the fear of God." In a church or a family or a

116

business or in any group relationship, each of us at some time is a leader and at some time a follower. Joe may be Bill's Sunday school teacher, but Bill may be the deacon chairman while Joe is a deacon. Joe may be manager of the softball team, while Bill may be Joe's choir director. One of the great necessities of a successful church is that each member realize the area in which he is a leader and the area in which he is a follower and learn to fill each position with grace, propriety and dispatch.

In any organization there are several groups of people, as follows:

1. *Followers of leaders.* **I Corinthians 4:10, "We are fools for Christ's sake, but ye are wise in Christ; we are weak, but ye are strong; ye are honourable, but we are despised."**

**I Corinthians 11:1, "Be ye followers of me, even as I also am of Christ."**

**Philippians 3:7, "But what things were gain to me, those I counted loss for Christ."**

In any organization this is the mass of the members. One of the great weaknesses rising on the scene in America is that so few people are trained to be followers. There is nothing undignified about being a follower. The follower is as important as the leader. Athletic contests are won by athletes who know how to follow and are trained to do so. America used to win wars when we trained our young men to be followers.

We say we believe in majority rule, and this is right. However, majority rule does not mean majority opinion. Following majority opinion is anarchy. Following majority rule is democracy. We choose people to lead us and make important decisions for us. An athletic team has a captain who calls the plays. The captain may be chosen by the team, but the captain calls the plays. On a football team, the quarterback calls the plays, or in some cases, the plays are called by the coach. There would be neither time nor proper organization if the team voted in the huddle what play to run. Imagine how long it would take for someone to make a motion that we throw a pass to the right wide receiver, someone else makes a motion that the fullback carries the ball through the center of the line, someone else makes a motion for a quick kick, and the quarterback asks then if there is any discussion! Each member of the team is allowed to discuss the motion. Then the quarterback calls for a vote, and the majority opinion decides on the play. A long time before the decision was made, the team would have been penalized for delay of game. You can't run a team that way; you can't run a nation that way, and you can't run a church that way (though this seems to be the way the Congress wants to run our foreign policy).

Once the leader is chosen, then the followers follow him. This does not mean that the leader is stronger than the follower; it simply means that in this particular area, he would have more ability to make the right decisions. Of course, the wise leader will often seek the advice and counsel of followers before making his decision, but the decision should be his. The follower should be loyal to that decision. This is the way wars are won, championships are won, and souls are won! Let the church choose a choir director and let him make the decisions for the choir. Don't saddle him with a music committee to nip at his heels. Let the choir follow.

Let the youth director make the decisions about the youth program. Choose one and follow him. Don't saddle him with a youth committee as an albatross around his neck.

In some churches it takes seven days for a committee of five to decide what kind and color of flowers to put on the communion table on Sunday. Let someone be chosen to be in charge of the flowers and send the committee out soul winning! If a business were run like the average church, it would go bankrupt. If a nation were run like the average church, it would go under. (In some ways it seems like our nation is run almost that way now.)

Choose a bus director and let that bus director make the decisions concerning the bus ministry. Do not appoint a bus committee to hinder the progress. Democracy is not voting on every issue but choosing our leaders and letting them lead. Of course, there are times for the need of a public referendum, but these are rare occasions and for special purposes.

A church should choose a pastor, vote him in democratically and then let him be the pastor. Do not appoint a committee to approve who fills the pulpit in his absence. Let the pastor choose. Do not have a board or a committee to approve his speaking engagements outside the church and to approve whatever advisory boards he sits on outside the church. Choose the pastor and let him be the pastor.

There are three words in the Bible all of which deal with the same office—pastor, elder and bishop. The title of pastor means that God's man should be careful to protect his people from false doctrine and heresy, as the shepherd protected his sheep from serpents and wild beasts and as he fed them. The title of elder signifies experience and wisdom as the pastor guides his people with the decisions of life. The title of bishop means overseer. A pastor is chosen democratically by the people, not to lead the church by majority opinion, but by wise leadership after having been chosen by majority vote.

Let no one mistake this for the pastor borrowing money for the church or building a building without a church vote, but the people should follow pastoral leadership. He is trained for the job and has been democratically voted to the job.

Years ago a deacon in a certain church informed me that the deacons of the church were not pleased with my preaching and asked if a meeting could be held to discuss my preaching. I agreed to such a meeting. The time was set for Monday night at 7:00 in one of the Sunday school rooms at the church. About 10:00 that night the deacon called me and asked me where I was. I said, "I'm at home."

He said, "Why didn't you come to the meeting?"

I said, "What meeting?"

He said, "You told me we could have a meeting to discuss your preaching," and I said, "You can. You can have a meeting every night if you want to discuss my preaching, but I won't be there. That's between me and God, not between me and the deacon board."

Years ago a deacon said to me, "Pastor, concerning your preaching. . . ."

I said, "Hold it. When we build a building, you get one vote. When we borrow money, you get one vote, but when I walk in the pulpit, you don't get no vote! Two and two is four; the sun rises in the east and sets in the west; the pope is a Catholic; and my preaching is between me and God."

This group that we call followers of leaders is only such in one particular phase of the work, but each organization needs people who love to follow and who are self-confident enough to yield, who are loyal and faithful.

The wise follower loves strength. He will be happy to follow strength and would be wise to study the leader to find the qualities he possesses in order for him to know those qualities if he is chosen someday to lead in some endeavor.

2. *Leaders of followers.* This is the second group.

1) *These people come from good followers.* No one will make a good leader unless he has first been a follower. He must know the heartbeat of the follower. He must have compassion and empathy toward the follower.

2) *He does not want power; he just wants to get things done.* He has no desire to lead or to have people subservient to him. He is lost in the necessity to accomplish a task. He realizes that he has been chosen to a place of leadership that will require him to lead in this task.

3) *He doesn't feel above the followers.* He feels that the position of leadership is not a position that is exalted above that of the follower. He realizes that somebody has to lead, and he has been chosen to do so. Perhaps another could have been chosen who could have done the job as well as he, but he realizes that he has been chosen for the job, so he accepts the responsibility, realizing that the followers are his equals, not his inferiors.

4) *He does not seek leadership.* This is one of the weaknesses of our system. Leadership is sought. The husband reminds his wife of **Ephesians 5:22, "Wives, submit yourselves unto your own husbands, as unto the Lord,"** and oftentimes that is his only right to be the leader. To be sure, the wife should obey

because the Bible says to, but far be it from me to believe that a weak man should take that Scripture and use it as a club! He should become strong and earn his wife's followship, convincing her that he is capable of leading. Now don't misunderstand me. She should follow whether he is capable or not. The Bible gives her that command, but at no place in the Bible does it say, "Husbands, command your wives. Husbands, boss your wives. Husbands, dictate to your wives." Why couldn't a husband be the kind of man that his wife would want to follow! What a delightful buffer this would give as **Ephesians 5:22** is carried out!

There is nothing more disgusting than for some little milquetoast to say in an effeminate way, "Matilda, you are supposed to obey me; the Bible says you are!"

Yes, Matilda, you should obey little milquetoast, but there is nothing in the Bible that says you have to enjoy it, and there is nothing in the Bible that says he deserves it!

There are few things more disgusting than for some little effeminate, papa-called, mama-fed, seminary-bred preacher to open the Bible to **Hebrews 13:7 and 17** and remind his people that they are supposed to follow him. **Hebrews 13:7, 17, "Remember them which have the rule over you, who have spoken unto you the Word of God: whose faith follow, considering the end of their conversation. Obey them that have the rule over you, and submit yourselves: for they watch for your souls, as they that must give account, that they may do it with joy, and not with grief: for that is unprofitable for you."** Now, it is true that they are supposed to follow, and the argument that I am presenting now gives no member a right to rebel against his pastor, but it is far better when God's man works to become capable of leadership! Through loving his people, working for their benefit, serving them, caring for them and ministering to them, he convinces them that he is capable of being their leader. They, in turn, follow him because they believe he is capable. Oh, yes, the letter of the law says that they are supposed to obey him, but how much more beautiful it is when

God's man loves his people and does not want to be a dictator and has no desire to rule them. He simply realizes that he has been chosen as their leader and feels that he is capable of doing it with God's help. He goes about doing his duty of leading them; and they, believing that he can lead them, follow him.

5) *He delivers followers to other leaders.* For example, if a man leads the church choir, he is a leader of followers, but he also has a pastor whom he is to follow. He is to lead the church choir to follow the pastor. If a man is the principal of a school which is operated by a church, he should increase the loyalty of those whom he leads to the pastor whom he follows. The wise and capable leader will realize that there are leaders above him, and he should present his followers as the most loyal followers of his leaders.

One of the sad things in our system is that so many of our national leaders have never led anything. So many of our congressmen graduated from college with a law degree or some other degree that put them in a position in business where they built nothing. They run for office on the basis of their charisma, charm and smile and are then elected as leaders. These are not officers who are commissioned on the battlefield because they have proven themselves as leaders, but rather chosen by a popular vote. These men sit in the halls of Congress, but they have never led a corporation; they have never built a business; they have never built a church; they simply went to a liberal university, kissed a few babies, shook several thousand hands, made a few television commercials and then assumed a place of leadership without ever having been a leader.

On the other hand, the President appoints his staff and his cabinet. He chooses men for his staff and cabinet who have been successful as leaders in America. He chooses men who have headed great corporations, men who have headed great armies, or men who have built empires. On one side you have the President's staff, chosen from the field of leadership, business and success. On the other side you have a Congress where many of its members have never built or led at all. We have seen in our generation how easy it is for the President's staff and cabinet to become impatient with the other side. The followers are leading leaders; novices are placed over successful men. Sometimes these men who have led in great corporations step over the line and make some mistakes. They immediately are investigated by the weaker ones who assert their right to leadership because the Constitution and the laws give it to them. They are right, but they are also weak. The temptation to do wrong was partially or maybe totally caused by their ineptness, and so they (like the husband who takes **Ephesians 5:22** and waves it in front of his wife and the pastor who takes **Hebrews 13:7 and 17** and waves it before his people) take the Constitution and wave it before the successful men who have crossed over a line because of their impatience in waiting for the inept ones to do something! Then a committee is formed so there can be a hearing where followship can interrogate leadership, where failure can interrogate success, and where weakness can interrogate strength!

It is not hard to understand why a strong man who is a leader steps across the line in an effort to do something to defend America from Communism, when the often inept and weak people sit on their hands while Communism invades our hemisphere.

We have seen in our day how colonels and admirals who have been trained at West Point and Annapolis and who have been taught how to be followers and how to be leaders are quizzed, disciplined and censored by men who were trained in liberal, undisciplined state universities and have been spawned by the permissive society and the situation ethics of our generation. While these weak men in strong positions point the finger of accusation at impatient and perhaps even erring strong men, somebody should point the finger at these men whose "do-nothingness" left the vacuum that was filled by the strong men who got out of bounds. Many of these men who have gotten out of bounds in their over-zealousness to keep America free, have

been pushed out of bounds or pulled out of bounds because no
one in bounds was doing anything! I am not condoning law-
breaking, nor am I condoning those who entice law-breaking.
There are laws in our country against rioting. There are also laws
in our country against those who incite a riot. There are laws in
our country against certain crimes, and there are also laws
against those who aid those crimes and incite those crimes. I
contend that the people who are letting Communism take over
America while they preach their doctrine of disarmament and
pacifism from college desks, senate seats, congressional ros-
trums and even pulpits are just as guilty as the patriots who are
excessive in their defense of America. I am not acquitting
anyone; I am simply indicting some others!

3. *Leaders of leaders.* **Deuteronomy 10:17, "For the Lord
your God is God of gods, and Lord of lords, a great God, a
mighty, and a terrible, which regardeth not persons, nor
taketh reward." I Timothy 6:15, "Which in His times He shall
shew, Who is the blessed and only Potentate, the King of kings,
and Lord of lords."**

It is very interesting that Jesus is called King of kings and Lord
of lords. Not only is He a King of subjects, but He is King over
kings. Not only is He a Lord over followers, but He is Lord over
lords. There are some people who have been chosen by leaders to
be their leaders. Pastors who lead churches have men to whom they
look for leadership. Men who lead corporations have men to whom
they look for leadership.

Here is where many churches stop growing. The pastor is a
leader of followers, and he takes the church as far as one leader can
take a church. Here is the place where he must become a leader of
leaders. He must choose men under him to lead different departments of the church. He must delegate to them responsibility and
some authority. He must learn to share with these leaders his people
and a part of his domain. Of course, these leaders whom he leads
should be fanatically loyal to the pastor and should not steal any of
the love that the people have for the pastor. When a church reaches a

certain size, its continued growth numerically will depend upon the ability of the pastor to become a leader of leaders. This is not easy. Some of the nice things the people have done for the pastor, they will now do for the other leaders. The pastor will have to share the banana puddings, the pecan pies and the pineapple upside-down cakes with those who work as his followers and as leaders of a portion of his people.

1) *This position should not be sought.* All true leadership should come from one who is so busy helping followers that they will want him to be the leader. This is true with the leader of leaders. He should be chosen by the leaders. This does not mean that he will be elected; it means that he just unknowingly becomes the kind of person to whom leaders look. The position is not sought; it just happens, or in some cases of organizational structure, he is chosen without his applying for the position.

Twenty-five years ago a man came to the First Baptist Church of Hammond and told me that he was a pastor and that he had heard of our church and wanted to learn something about the ministry of our church. We put him in a guest room, kept him for the entire week and let each staff member talk to him for one hour. His ministry was transformed. He went back to his church in the western part of our nation, and his church was transformed. He told a friend what had happened to him. The friend contacted me and asked if he could come and spend a week learning from our staff members concerning our work. We allowed him to do so. He had a friend, and he came. He had a friend who came, and he had a friend who came, until we were spending far too much time individually with pastors each coming to spend a week. I got with the staff and we decided we would have one week and announce it so that all who wanted to come could come. It was to be a one-time situation. We simply got word around the country that any pastor who wanted to come and spend a week and spend an hour with each of our staff members could do so, but it would all happen at the same time. To our total shock, 167 pastors from 19 states came. When that week was over we never intended to do it again. Then requests came from all over America concerning a repeat. Other pastors wanted to spend the same week, so we did it the second year. For twenty-five consecutive years we have had what we call our nationwide Pastors' School, where pastors and Christian workers come from all over America and from around the world. Five to six thousand come each year to spend a week of training. (Last year over 6,000 came from 48 states and 19 foreign countries.) We start on Monday night, have sessions all day Tuesday and Tuesday night, all day Wednesday and Wednesday night, all day Thursday and Thursday night, and most of Friday.

Now I did not sit in my office one day and say, "I would like to become a leader of leaders, and I've got to figure out some way where I can have leaders to come here so I can be their leader." It never works that way! The position of becoming a leader of leaders just happens.

The truth is, I don't enjoy being an administrator or an executive. I was reared a poor boy and had no intention at all of ever being any kind of an executive. In fact, I didn't like that word. I was pastoring the Miller Road Baptist Church of Garland, Texas. We had about 300 in attendance, and I was doing everything! I was leading the choir, printing the church bulletin, turning on the lights and the heat, typing letters to the visitors and new members, mimeographing the Sunday school outline for the teachers and officers in addition to my pastoral duties. I hired a secretary, and I had a hard time relinquishing the things I was doing. This little secretary's name was Jo Strickland. She did me a favor, for which I could never adequately repay her. One day this little short gal said to me, "Pastor, I have been a secretary for an insurance executive, and you need to learn how to delegate responsibility and be an executive." I told her I didn't even like the word. I wasn't a big shot, and I didn't want to become one! She looked at me and very sincerely said, "Pastor, I believe you could be a great preacher someday, but you are going to limit yourself if you don't learn to delegate responsibility. You will

never be able to build a big church unless you can administrate."
(What she was saying was it was time for me to become a leader
of leaders!) She looked up at me and said, "Say this to me: 'I am
an executive!' "

I don't know why I did, but I said it.

She said, "Say it over ten times," and to my shock I did it.
Every morning when I came to work, she met me at the door and
required me to look down at her and say that phrase ten times: "I
am an executive! I am an executive! I am an executive! I am an
executive! I am an executive! I am an executive! I am an
executive! I am an executive! I am an executive! I am an
executive!" What she was doing was helping me to become a
leader of leaders. This was a pivotal time in my ministry. Every
leader reaches the place on the ladder of success where he can no
longer continue to prosper or grow by just being a leader of
followers. He must become a leader of leaders.

2) *The leader of leaders must learn to delegate.* This is hard
for a zealous leader to do. Something that has helped me tremendously is the awareness that if I have ten men who work for me,
and if I think I can do the job that each is doing better than he is
doing it, I still can get more done by letting him do his own job.
Let's suppose I have ten men working for me, and that each of
those ten men can only do his job 90% as effectively as I could
do it. (Of course, this is not always the case. Some of the men
who work for me can do their jobs far better than I could do
them.) However, it dawned on me one day that I would get more
done by letting these men do their jobs, even though they could
do them only 90% as well as I could. It is simply a matter of
mathematics. I cannot do all the jobs, so I would rather have 10
men working at 90% efficiency than one man working at 100%
efficiency. It is a mathematical fact of 900 to 100, so the leader
of leaders must learn to delegate!

3) *The leader of leaders must learn to share glory.* He must
honor the leaders whom he leads. He must exalt them in the
minds of the followers.

Let me stop to say this: The leaders who are led by the leader of leaders should not demand this kind of treatment. This is an exhortation to the leader of leaders to share the glory; it is not an exhortation or a license given to the leaders who follow the leader of leaders to demand such glory. God would not honor this kind of a spirit. However, the wise leader of leaders will give credit where credit is due, honor where honor is due and will exalt in the presence of the followers those leaders whom he leads.

4) *The leader of leaders must learn to share the spoils with the leaders who follow him.*

The first time I ever had a leader under me was in the early 1950's. His name was Bob Keyes. Until that time, I had gotten all the cakes, pies, turnip greens, green beans and other nice things that people give to and do for the pastor. The first week that Bob Keyes worked for me, I went by his house. He and his family were eating a meal of freshly-cooked vegetables. I walked in, smelled the meal, coveted the vegetables and told them it sure smelled good and looked good.

Bob said, "Yes, these are fresh out of the garden."

That green-eyed monster came inside my heart and I said, "You don't have a garden! Whose garden?"

He said, "Well, some members of the church brought these by to us today," and I said to myself, "They didn't bring me any!" I was learning that I must share with my followers the leader whom I was leading.

Evangelist Jim Lyons at one time was my associate pastor. One cold winter day I was backing out of my driveway (it is a curved driveway), and I got off of the drive into a snowbank. I tried to get out and couldn't. I gunned the engine, went forward a bit, backward a bit, forward a bit, backward a bit, and then I smelled something! I knew what I had done. I had burned up the transmission. There I was—sitting in a snowbank with no transmission, realizing that it would cost me hundreds of dollars to have it fixed or replaced, when suddenly Jim Lyons and his wife drove up in front of our house. He shouted, "Preacher, are you having trouble?"

I replied something like this, "No, Jim. I just come out here every day and try to find a snowbank where I can put my car and burn up my transmission!"

Jim said, "Well, why don't you get some snow tires?"

I said, "I don't have any money to buy snow tires. Do you have snow tires?"

He said, "Yes."

I said, "Where did you get them?"

He said, "The Cliftons gave them to me."

Oh boy, that green-eyed monster came to me again! I was learning again that in order to have leaders whom I lead, I must share with them the spoils from the followers.

5) *The leader of leaders must oftentimes accept being misunderstood.* His life is a lonely life. The people to whom he was once close are now led on a personal basis by other leaders whom he leads. He will be misunderstood. This goes back to what President Harry Truman said, "If you can't stand the heat, don't get in the kitchen." A part of the heat of being a leader of leaders is sharing the glory and the spoils with the leaders whom the leader leads.

6) *The leader of leaders must oftentimes give up closeness that he would like to have.* I would like to be as close to our young people as our youth director is, but I cannot. The church is too big. I would like to be as close to our senior citizens as the director of our senior citizens ministry is, but I cannot. The church is too big. I would like to be as close to those in the hospital as my associate pastor John Colsten is, but I cannot. The church is too big. I would like to be as close to the football team at Hammond Baptist High School as the coach is, but I cannot. The church is too big. I would like to be as close to the school teachers as the principals are, but I cannot. The church is too big. I would like to be as close to the bus workers as the bus directors are, but I cannot. The church is too big. I would like to be as close

to the college students at Hyles-Anderson College as the teachers are, but I cannot. The church is too big. This is a price to pay, but it is well worth it in order to reach more people. This means the leader of leaders must walk with God in a closer way than do his followers and leaders whom he leads.

When the Israelites came into the promised land, God divided the land and gave a portion to 11 of the 12 tribes. The tribe of Levi received no such portion of land. They asked God what their portion would be. He replied, "I am your portion." This is true in a church concerning a pastor who has become a leader of leaders.

7) *The leader of leaders must be willing to be second or third in the minds of some of the people.* I have a large staff. There are many men who work for me. I often tell my congregation that I do not expect them to put me first on their love list; just put me somewhere on the list. In the minds of some I will be number one; in the minds of others I will be number two or number three, number four, number five. That doesn't matter, as long as I am on the list. I simply ask them to love me; not to love me first or love me most. There are some people in my church who love Brother John Colsten more than they love me. That's all right as long as they love me. There are some who love Brother Roy Moffitt more than they love me. There are some who love Brother Elmer Fernandez more than they love me. There are some who have more love for other members of the staff such as Bob Auclair, Eddie Lapina, Keith McKinney, Bill Schutt, Ray Young, Wendell Evans, Mike Sisson, Greg Weber, Tom Vogel, etc. I want some people to put each of these men first (though the loyal man will not seek such love for himself).

Leaders are reading this chapter. Do not seek to be a leader of leaders in non-organizational areas. Some doctors simply are highly respected and regarded by other doctors and become leaders of leaders. Some lawyers just happen to rise to a place of similar respectability. The same is true with preachers, and with leaders in every other field.

However, in an organizational structure such as a church, the wise pastor will have people who follow him, but who lead segments of the congregation in various ministries. The work of the church can be multiplied many times if such a relationship can be one of grace, love, admiration and acceptance.

4. *A follower of followers.* **Matthew 15:14, "Let them alone: they be blind leaders of the blind. And if the blind lead the blind, both shall fall into the ditch."** In every church, and for that matter, in every organization, there are people who do not follow the designated leadership. Some of these people perhaps are jealous of strength because they are almost always weak themselves. These people may be those who wanted to lead and failed, and so they do not like to follow leadership. These are people who are critics of leaders. They usually hate strong people, or at least, they do not like them. They are often one-issue people and have one doctrine that they advocate, one project that they promote, or one conviction that they advocate above others. These are they who often have tried to lead and failed, and so they pick away at leadership. No matter what organization they are in, they do not follow. If they are choir members, they do not cooperate with the choir director. They do not come to choir practice, and if they do, they try to aggravate the choir director. If they are bus captains, they will not cooperate in the bus meetings, either by causing a problem when they are there or by not attending the meetings at all (which is a blessing to the director!).

The tragic thing is the fact that there are many who follow these followers. They preach their sermons from restaurant tables as they promote their opposition to the chosen leadership. They are followers of followers. How tragic this is! These followers are often lovely people who are misled by those whose only ability to lead is to lead someone against the leader. Their only achievement is to criticize achievers, and their only success is to lead others in opposition to the successful. These followers usually are lovely people who are misled by a warm personality of a follower who wants to lead and can lead only those whom he can get disgruntled.

Let God's people beware of followers whose only leadership is that of rebellion, criticism and division.

All over America churches have been split by these followers who lead followers, and so many of these followers who follow followers have gone with them to start other churches, and all over America there are little groups of people who are living in failure because they have followed a follower instead of a leader. Many young people have lost confidence in leadership because of these misguided souls. Thank God for those who are followers, but let all followers be careful to follow those who are leaders and not those whose only accomplishment is to fight leadership and to gather around themselves a few followers who became disgruntled and usually, sad to say, come to naught.

5. *Followers of leaders of leaders.* This is that type of Christian who wants to follow the famous name. He will support financially a leader of leaders, perhaps through some kind of nationwide ministry, but he is not willing to follow and support his own leader, the faithful pastor of his own church. He is enchanted by a personality, infected with hero worship, and will often drive hundreds of miles to hear a famous name but is seldom interested in supporting the leader nearest him. It is also true that if this follower of a leader of leaders were to become acquainted on a day-to-day basis with his hero, he would probably become disenchanted. He can follow only at a distance and not up close.

One of these such followers of the leader of leaders came to me when I was preaching in a distant state. He told me that he certainly was pleased to hear me and that he wished that they had a seasoned pastor at their church instead of the young man that God had given them. He was much chagrined because his young pastor made foolish mistakes. He tried to build himself in my estimation (and failed) by telling me that he wished he had a pastor like me that would not be susceptible to mistakes of youth.

The next night when I stood to speak, I told of this man's statement to me (though I did not imply at all or even give a hint as to the man's name). I then proceeded to tell the audience of a mistake that I had made just a few years before, after I had been in

Hammond for about 20 years. Our church is a downtown church. We have purchased many buildings in the downtown area of Hammond. We bought a department store building, a drug store, a restaurant, four furniture companies, a lodge building, four small stores, a cleaners, a barber shop, a beauty shop and several apartment buildings.

On this particular occasion we had purchased a three-story building behind our auditorium. One night at deacons' meeting a motion was made and seconded that we tear down the building and use it for parking. One deacon included in his motion that we appoint a committee to have the building torn down. I immediately suggested that it was foolish to appoint a committee; I could take care of it. All I had to do was simply call the demolition company and tell them to tear the building down. The deacons agreed to do so.

I did call the demolition company, but I failed to give them proper instructions! They did tear the building down that we had purchased. They also tore down the three-story building next door that we did not own. Boy, was I ever shocked and surprised to find that we had torn down a building that we did not own! How would you like to come to work some morning and find your building gone—especially if you were the owner of the building! I called a meeting of my deacons for Saturday night. They did not know what had happened. I immediately started the meeting by saying, "Fellows, did you ever hear of the Scripture that says, 'If a man asks you to go a mile, go with him two'? Well, I had the building torn down just as you requested, but I also tore the one down next door." I told them that I would not blame them if they asked the church to fire me.

One deacon kiddingly said, "Well, we don't pay much; we don't expect much!"

I kiddingly replied, "One more crack out of you, and your house comes down tonight!"

A deacon across the room shouted to him in jest, "Don't worry, he'll get the one next door instead!"

One deacon stood and said, "You've been my pastor for all these years, and I love you and am going to follow you regardless. As far as I'm concerned you can tear down the whole city of Hammond, and you are still my preacher."

I then began to think of other buildings that could come down! How about the adult bookstore? How about the movie houses and the liberal churches? (Of course, this was all in humor.)

One by one our deacons stood to tell me of their love and loyalty. What could have been serious trouble turned into a little revival meeting.

I told this story to the people where I was preaching and reminded them that leaders of leaders make foolish mistakes and errors just like leaders do and that older more seasoned preachers are prone to mistakes also.

What I am saying is this: The member of the church should follow the pastor—his own pastor. The pastor may not be as glamorous as some nationally-known figure, but he is God's man for that place, and he should be followed. Yes, we ought to love the leaders of leaders, but we also ought to love, appreciate and follow that one that God has given us to lead us on a local scale.

Are you a follower of leaders? Then be a faithful, loyal one. Are you a leader of followers? Then be a considerate, compassionate one. Are you a leader of leaders? Then be an unselfish, sharing one. Are you a follower of followers? Then turn from following discontents and disgruntles, and follow God's chosen leader. Are you a follower of leaders of leaders? Then add to that your followship of your own leader. May God make us to be in any capacity what He would have us be.

# Chapter 15

# My Ten Commandments
# When Sinned Against

I refuse to allow the existence of my happiness to depend upon the actions of others. I will allow the degree of my happiness to depend on the actions of others. I will not allow myself to be unhappy or to lose my joy because of the behavior of someone else. I will allow myself to have joy and happiness only because of conditions within my ability to determine. If my joy is dependent upon your treatment of me, I can have joy only when you decide for me to have joy. If my joy is dependent upon my treatment of you, then I may have that joy any time I choose. If my joy is dependent upon my relationship with God, then I may have joy when I choose to do so. If my joy is dependent upon my service for others, then I may have that joy any time I choose to serve others. So the presence of my joy must not be dependent upon the actions of others and their behavior toward me. However, the degree of that joy may be so determined. In other words, I will not let you make me happy, but I will let you make me happier.

Even in church life the carnal sometimes prevails over the spiritual, and Christians sin against each other. The purpose of this chapter is to give instruction to the one who is sinned against. For years I have had what I call, "My Ten Commandments When Sinned Against." These are ten things that I do when I find that someone has sinned against me.

Before entering the discussion of these ten commandments, we must make it clear that there is no selfish purpose or motive in-

volved in these actions and reactions. The one supreme motive is
TO RESTORE THE ONE WHO HAS SINNED AGAINST ME. I
must look upon him as I would look upon any Christian who has
committed any other sin. I must be grieved because it has strained
his relationship with God. I must not allow my grief to exist
because I have been wounded or offended. The truth is, if I love the
Word of God and the God of the Word as I should, there is no way
that I can be offended. **Psalm 119:165, "Great peace have they
which love Thy law: and nothing shall offend them."**

As we enter into these ten commandments, we will always keep
before us that our purpose is to restore the offender. If you have
sinned against me, I want you to have the joy that has been taken
from you because of your offense. My purpose is to help you and,
by God's grace, to help you be restored!

*COMMANDMENT 1. I will have forgiveness in readiness before
you sin against me.* **Ephesians 4:32, "And be ye kind one to
another, tenderhearted, forgiving one another, even as God for
Christ's sake hath forgiven you."** I will always keep a reservoir of
forgiveness so that it can be used immediately when sinned
against. I will not allow myself the indulgence of the time that often
transpires between being sinned against and offering forgiveness.
That forgiveness will always be available and in abundant readiness
immediately when the sin against me has been committed.

*COMMANDMENT 2. I will not impute your sin to you.* **Ephesians 4:32, "And be ye kind one to another, tenderhearted,
forgiving one another, even as God for Christ's sake hath
forgiven you."** Notice here that I am to forgive those who offend
me just exactly as God forgives those who offend Him. God not
only forgives our sins, but He also justifies us. In other words, God
keeps in readiness "justified forgiveness," which means that God
does not charge us with the sin. He does not record it against us.
When a Christian is saved, he is justified by the faith which is
placed in Christ. **Romans 5:1, "Therefore being justified by
faith, we have peace with God through our Lord Jesus Christ."**
If, therefore, I forgive you as God for Christ's sake has forgiven me,

I must not only forgive you, but I must not charge you with the offense. In my mind, you never sinned against me. I call that "justified forgiveness." Not only do I forgive you for what you've done, but I do not record what you have done. I do not think of you as one forgiven, but I think of you as one who has not sinned at all.

*COMMANDMENT 3. I will grieve for you, but not for what you have done to me.* I will not grieve because I have an enemy; I will grieve because you are an enemy. I will not grieve because I have been sinned against; I will grieve because you have sinned. I want you to have a good relationship with Christ. I want you to have peace. I want you to have fullness of joy, and you can have none of these when being offensive, so my grief is not for the wounded but for the wounder. My grief is not for the criticized but for the critic. My grief is not for myself, though I certainly want your love. My grief is for you because I want the best for you, and you cannot have the best when you have sinned against another.

*COMMANDMENT 4. I will do all that I can to help you remedy your situation.* I will not retaliate. I will not be critical of you. I will not even share with others what you have done against me. My entire course of action will be that of seeking your restoration. I want you restored to fellowship with Christ. I want your joy restored, your peace restored and your happiness restored, so nothing that I do in the following commandments will be done to try to hurt you but to help you. I will not want for your hurt unless God chooses that method to bring you back to Himself. I will want the best for you and will do all that I can for that best to come your way.

*COMMANDMENT 5. I will ask God to let me suffer for you.* **I Corinthians 6:6-8, "But brother goeth to law with brother, and that before the unbelievers. Now therefore there is utterly a fault among you, because ye go to law one with another. Why do ye not rather take wrong? why do ye not rather suffer yourselves to be defrauded? Nay, ye do wrong, and defraud, and that your brethren."** Not only will my forgiveness be justified forgiveness, but it will be vicarious forgiveness. I will ask God to punish me instead of you if that can best serve to bring about your restoration. I must not forget that the entire purpose of these commandments is for you to be restored, and I must do all I can to bring that restoration about. Isn't that the way that Jesus cared for our sins? He bore the suffering for us vicariously. Do not forget that I am to forgive as God forgives, so if God took upon Himself the suffering for our sins, even so I must take upon myself the suffering for your sins if God will but let me do so. I have forgiven you. I have offered you with that forgiveness a justified forgiveness, and now I offer to you a vicarious forgiveness.

Certainly by now I want you to be restored. However, if you are not yet restored, I must continue to do what I can to help you find the peace you once had and the joy you once knew in Christ. If at any time while I am obeying these ten commandments, you are restored, then the use of the balance of the commandments will not be necessary. However, if having had forgiveness in readiness for you, having offered you justified forgiveness, having grieved for you, having decided to do all that I can to remedy your situation and having offered you a vicarious forgiveness with a willingness to suffer your penalty, I find that you are not yet restored, I must proceed to the next commandment.

*COMMANDMENT 6. I will turn you over to God for justice.* **Romans 12:17-20, "Recompense to no man evil for evil. Provide things honest in the sight of all men. If it be possible, as much as lieth in you, live peaceably with all men. Dearly beloved, avenge not yourselves, but rather give place unto wrath: for it is written, Vengeance is Mine; I will repay, saith the Lord. Therefore if thine enemy hunger, feed him; if he thirst, give him drink: for in so doing thou shalt heap coals of fire on his head."** Do not forget that this justice that I seek for you from God is for your restoration.

Far too often I have heard this passage explained in a way to describe the Christian as one who wants his offender to be hurt and that God is certainly a better executer of this hurt than we can be. So it is taught that if you really want to hurt somebody, let God do it, and even blessing those that curse us is supposedly done in an effort to heap coals of fire upon his head. What a tragic teaching! How sad it is for us to teach God's people to be good to somebody because it will make them feel bad, to love somebody because it will make them hurt. God teaches no such thing! We must never forget that the purpose for all of this is for restoration. We are not trying to see to it that someone gets punished for his sin unless that punishment will help to restore him.

We simply treat him with love. If he hates us, we love him. If he despises us, we pray for him. If he does ill to us, we do good to him and turn him over to the Lord for justice, hoping that that justice will lead him to restoration. We would rather that he not suffer at all, but if God chooses to use the tool of suffering to bring him back to joy, peace and restoration, we will be happy for that, but we will never be happy because he suffers. We are pleased only if that suffering leads to restoration. All of this must be remedial.

The word "vengeance" here has to do with justice, and the justice has to do with chastening, and the chastening we hope and trust will lead to repentance, and repentance will lead to a restoration of fellowship with God, and a restoration of that fellowship will lead the offender to regain his joy and peace.

Why should we want to use the same tactics he used? Why should we borrow Satan's weapons to punish those who have punished us? Do not forget! The purpose of these ten commandments is restoration. If forgiving immediately brings it about, Commandment 1 is all that is necessary. If that fails, we will offer justified forgiveness and let our offender know that we are not charging the sin to him at all. Then we will attempt restoration by grieving for him and then doing all we can to remedy his situation, and then by asking God to let us suffer for him, and when all of those commandments have failed, we then turn him over to the Lord so God may use justice upon him in order that that justice may lead him back to his original fellowship and relationship with his God. If our brother is still not restored, we go to the next commandment.

*COMMANDMENT 7. I will turn you over to the Lord for chastening.* **Hebrews 12:10-12, "For they verily for a few days chastened us after their own pleasure; but He for our profit, that we might be partakers of His holiness. Now no chastening for the present seemeth to be joyous, but grievous: nevertheless afterward it yieldeth the peaceable fruit of righteousness unto them which are exercised thereby. Wherefore lift up the hands which hang down, and the feeble knees."** In other words, I will ask God to chasten you, but I must remember through it all that I am not wanting you to be hurt. I am wanting you to be restored, and if asking God to chasten you leads to this restoration, I will be pleased to do so. I will not enjoy your suffering or your pain any more than a loving parent enjoys the suffering of the child he is spanking, but I will wish for it if it will lead to your restoration. Of course, the word "chastening" implies training or educating. God does not punish His children for sin. His measures of inflicting pain upon us are not vindictive. They are punitive and corrective and done in love. The loving parent has in mind training his child, improving his child, educating his child, and in doing this, oftentimes must use the inflicting of pain. Never forget, the purpose is remedial!

I would much prefer that my forgiveness in itself would bring you to restoration. I would love for my justifying you as if you had never sinned against me to accomplish this. I would hope that a long time before we get to Commandment 7, you have been restored to fellowship with your God and have received once again the sweet peace and joy that comes with that fellowship, and only for your restoration to that place will I want you to be chastened.

As has been implied, God does not punish Christians; He chastens them. Now it may look the same way and it may, as a fact, be the same action. God may do exactly the same thing to a saved man that He does to an unsaved man, but to the unsaved it is punishment; to the saved man it is chastening. He chastens those whom He loves. To the one who is not His child, He may inflict punishment for sin, and though He may use that same act upon the Christian, it will not be punishment; it will be chastening. It will be done for training, for educating and for restoring His child to Himself.

Certainly we trust that by now the one who has sinned against us has been restored, but if not, there is another commandment.

*COMMANDMENT 8. I will turn you over to Satan for the destruction of the flesh.* **I Corinthians 5:1-5, "It is reported commonly that there is fornication among you, and such fornication as is not so much as named among the Gentiles, that one should have his father's wife. And ye are puffed up, and have not rather mourned, that he that hath done this deed might be taken away from among you. For I verily, as absent in body, but present in spirit, have judged already, as though I were present, concerning him that hath so done this deed. In the name of our Lord Jesus Christ, when ye are gathered together, and my spirit, with the power of our Lord Jesus Christ, to deliver such an one unto Satan for the destruction of the flesh, that the spirit may be saved in the day of the Lord Jesus."** Notice especially the first part of **verse 5, "to deliver such an one unto Satan for the destruction of the flesh,"** but don't stop there. Notice the rest of the verse, **"that the spirit may be saved in the day of the Lord Jesus."** It is folly for us to think that we are to say, "I tried to hurt him, and God tried to hurt him; now Devil, you hurt him." This is contrary to the whole spirit of the Bible. It is contrary to the attitude of God toward His children. God is not talking here about a judgmental deliverance of the sinner to the executioner. God is simply saying He will exhaust every measure in order to restore the offender to Himself.

Another error that is taught concerning this subject is that this means we are to turn someone over to the Devil and say, "Devil, kill him!" That is not taught here. Notice that the destruction is of the flesh, the destruction of the carnality, the destruction of the methods that caused him to sin. God oftentimes will let the Devil use his weapons on us, but even then the purpose is for our restoration. I do not come with a vindictive spirit in a hateful manner and almost with delight saying to the Devil, "You can have him. Kill him."

Turn to **I Timothy 1:19, 20, "Holding faith, and a good con-science; which some having put away concerning faith have made shipwreck. Of whom is Hymenaeus and Alexander; whom I have delivered unto Satan, that they may learn not to blaspheme."** Now notice especially **verse 20** where the Apostle says, **"whom I have delivered unto Satan, THAT THEY MAY LEARN not to blaspheme."** What is the purpose of turning one over to Satan? THAT HE MAY LEARN. This is the same as the chastening in Commandment 7. Even in this action we are seeking restoration. This one, like all the commandments above, is for the good of the offender that he might be led to know once again the peace and joy he knew before he sinned against me. Even in turning him over to Satan for the destruction of the flesh, I am still interested in corrective measures, or as John Calvin said concerning this truth, "for medicinal purposes." This is just another medicine that I will use in an effort for your spirit to be healed.

*COMMANDMENT 9. I will bless you, do good to you, pray for you and love you.* **Matthew 5:43, 44, "Ye have heard that it hath been said, "Thou shalt love thy neighbour, and hate thine enemy. But I say unto you, Love your enemies, bless them that curse you, do good to them that hate you, and pray for them which despitefully use you, and persecute you." Romans 12:20, 21, "Therefore if thine enemy hunger, feed him; if he thirst, give him drink: for in so doing thou shalt heap coals of fire on his head. Be not overcome of evil, but overcome evil with good."** I will not combat hatred with hatred, but I will combat hatred with love. I will not combat cursing with cursing, but I will combat cursing with blessing. I will not combat spite with spite, but I will combat spite with prayer, hoping still that the weapons of love, blessing, prayer and kindness will lead to your restoration because I love you. I loved you before you sinned against me. I love you more now because you need me more. You need my love more, my blessings more, my prayer more.

*COMMANDMENT 10. I will not socialize with you.* **I Cor-inthians 5:9-11, "I wrote unto you in an epistle not to company** with fornicators: yet not altogether with the fornicators of this world, or with the covetous, or extortioners, or with idolaters; for then must ye needs go out of the world. But now I have written unto you not to keep company, if any man that is called a brother be a fornicator, or covetous, or an idolater, or a railer, or a drunkard, or an extortioner; with such an one no not to eat." II Thessalonians 3:14, "And if any man obey not our word by this epistle, note that man, and have no company with him, that he may be ashamed."

Perhaps you are saying, "Now you are showing some hatred at last. You finally came to a commandmnt that is vindicative!" No, quite to the contrary. Even this commandment is remedial and medicinal as a last resort. I will not socialize with you, hoping that you will miss my fellowship. Of course, I am commanded in the Scriptures above not to socialize with you, but even this is an effort for you to be restored. I trust that you will miss my fellowship and that my withdrawal from socializing with you will lead to your restoration.

This does not mean that I will not be nice to you. I will speak to you, I will help you, I will bless you, I will pray for you, I will be kind to you, I will be gracious to you, I will feed you if you are hungry, I will clothe you if you are cold. I will do anything I can for you, but I will not socialize with you because I am commanded not to do so and because again I am using a tool that I trust and pray unto God will restore you to fellowship with God and to your relationship with Him that brought you peace and joy, and as a blessed by-product, restore you to myself.

In conclusion, if you are my enemy and if you have sinned against me, I love you and I want you restored. The commandments that I have listed above are simply different medicines in the apothecary that I trust will heal your wounded spirit and bring you back to your God and to me, your friend. Perhaps these medicines taste progressively worse, and I certainly trust that before the more drastic ones are needed, you will be restored. I do not want you to suffer. I do not want you to hurt, but far above that, I want you restored to your God and to your joy. If therefore, a little suffering and a little pain will be remedial and medicinal, I will want it for you, not so you can hurt, but so the joy of fellowship you once knew can be yours, because you see, my dear enemy, I love you!

# Chapter 16

# Choosing Your Friends in the Church

In any church, there are several groups of people. That fact is the very purpose of the writing of this book. There is a group of the weak, a group of the fallen, a group of the strong, a group of the critical, etc. Of course, this is true in any group of people or cross section of society. Each Christian must decide which group he wants to join and who his choice of friends will be.

1. *You must first decide what you want to be.* Do you want to be strong? Do you want to be weak? Do you want to be fallen? Do you want to be critical? Do you want to be loyal? Do you want to be disloyal? This decision must precede all others.

2. *You must then associate yourself with the group of people who are like that.* You will be like your associations. You will not regularly associate with the disloyal and continue to be loyal. Neither will you regularly associate yourself with the loyal and continue to be disloyal. You will not regularly associate yourself with the strong and continue to be weak. You will not regularly associate yourself with the weak and continue to be strong.

You have first decided what you want to be. Then you have found the group that is composed of people like your goal, and you have associated yourself with them.

3. *Do not try to copy them, and do not try not to copy them.* All of us have heard sermons innumerable, warning us not to be somebody else, but to be ourselves. Christian colleges especially are bombarded with such statements, and there is a bit of truth in the

statement, but it does not go far enough. Just as the Christian is not to TRY to copy his associates, even so he should not NOT TRY to copy his associates. The mistake is the TRYING. Get with the right crowd. Do not force becoming like them. Do not attempt to keep your uniqueness; just be with them. Of course, we are assuming that you have chosen the right crowd. In other words, do not try to be anyone else, and do not NOT TRY to be anyone else.

It was my fortune as a young preacher in my late 20's to begin associating with and preaching with the greatest preachers of the former generation. As a young man not yet 30 years of age, I began preaching on the same platform with such men as Dr. John R. Rice, Dr. Bob Jones, Sr., Dr. R. G. Lee, Dr. Lee Roberson, Dr. Lester Roloff, Dr. Bill Rice, Dr. Ford Porter and others. I made no attempt to copy these men. I tried to be myself, but I made no attempt not to copy these men. I simply was with them, hoping that some of their greatness would rub off on me. I watched them preach. I watched them walk. I watched them sit on the platform. I prayed with them. I preached with them. I studied with them. I traveled with them, and on occasion, I even shared the same motel room with them. It would have been a tragedy for me to have copied any of them. It would have been just as tragic for me to have refused to allow them to influence me. Occasionally one of my members will come to me after a message and say, "You reminded me today of Dr. John R. Rice." It is not unusual for someone to inform me that they saw Dr. Bill Rice in me while I was preaching. The same can be said of Dr. Bob Jones, Sr., Dr. G. B. Vick, Dr. Roloff and others. When I was a younger preacher one of my members told me one time that they could always tell on Wednesday night with whom I had preached on Monday and Tuesday. I assure you there was no purposeful effort for me to preach like any one of these men. Neither was there a purposeful effort for me not to preach like any one of these men. I simply let them influence me by osmosis, not encouraging or fighting that influence.

The wise Christian will first decide what he wants to be like. Then he will associate himself with that crowd. If you want to be a critical person, do it on purpose. Find the critical crowd and run with them. You will be successful in your goal. If you want to be a weak Christian, do it on purpose. Find the weak Christians and run with them. Likewise, if you want to be a strong Christian, do it on purpose. Find the strong Christians and run with them. Once you have decided what you want to be and have found the crowd that can influence you to be that, get with that crowd and relax!

4. *Weakness and strength should never be equal.* **II Corinthians 6:14-17, "Be ye not unequally yoked together with unbelievers: for what fellowship hath righteousness with unrighteousness? and what communion hath light with darkness? And what concord hath Christ with Belial? or what part hath he that believeth with an infidel? And what agreement hath the temple of God with idols? for ye are the temple of the living God: as God hath said, I will dwell in them, and walk in them; and I will be their God, and they shall be My people. Wherefore come out from among them, and be ye separate, saith the Lord, and touch not the unclean thing; and I will receive you."** Notice especially the words, **"Be ye not unequally YOKED together with unbelievers."** Now a yoke holds two together. It may be a team of mules, a team of oxen, but a yoke is made for a pair. God does not want His people pairing off one-on-one with the weak. One critic plus one non-critic equals two critics. One gossip plus one non-gossip equals two gossips. One disloyal plus one loyal equals two disloyals. God does not want us to give the weak Christian the home-court advantage. A strong Christian will not change the crowd that is weak. However, a crowd of strong Christians can change a weak Christian.

I think there is a real weakness taught in many of our fundamental circles, and that is what we normally call the "buddy system." I do not think the buddy system is a good idea. In other words, one stronger Christian becomes a buddy with a weaker Christian in order to strengthen him. Most of the time this will weaken the strong Christian. The wise plan is to have a group of strong Christians with the weak Christian. Have the weak Christian join five strong Christians so that strength can be in the majority.

5. *Do not choose a crowd or a person that is not what you would like to become and then decide what good you can learn from them.* The truth is that we do not know what we learn. We do not choose what we learn. There are so many things we learn that we do not know we are learning.

I am thinking of a dear friend of mine who has pastored for many years. He decided to go to different pastors' schools, conferences, conventions, etc. of all persuasions to choose the best of each. He chose one such meeting conducted by a very well-known pastor who would not be considered by fundamentalists to be fundamental. He went to this meeting to choose the good and refuse the bad. Since this is impossible, he was influenced by the charisma of the pastor and began to embrace and endorse things that were contrary to his former ministry. He gave the other side home-court advantage, and in so doing, accepted practices that previously he never would have accepted!

Now let us suppose that same brother had come to the Pastors' School at First Baptist Church of Hammond where the fundamental position has home-court advantage. If the same statements contrary to his former position had been made by someone in conversation, he would have refuted them, at least in his own mind, and certainly would not have embraced or endorsed them. However, he allowed himself to be outnumbered by weakness and in so doing, accepted things he never would have accepted otherwise. Do not let strength go to the weak group to try to help, but form a strong group to invite the weak one that he may be helped. DO NOT GIVE WEAKNESS THE HOME-COURT ADVANTAGE.

6. *Remember, it is the personality that changes you.* The same thing can be done by television. When one watches a television program, he is giving the program home-court advantage. The television personality is not brought into your living room; you are brought into his setting. In your mind, you are sitting with him at his place. You are in his crowd. This is why television can be so deadly! For example, when you watch a talk show whose guests

hold an opinion contrary to yours, you are allowing yourself to come under the influence of their charisma in their setting with their having the home-court advantage. If that same person came to your home with the same philosophy, you would not allow it! This is because when he comes to your home, you then have the home-court advantage, and you refuse to be influenced in such a manner. This is the power of television. The world decides the crowd with whom you will run, and likewise decides the conditions and environment surrounding you and those who want to influence you.

The wise Christian will decide what he wants to be and will avoid watching personalities on television who are not what he wants to be.

The same is true with radio. If you want to be a separated, fundamentalist Christian, then listen only to separated, fundamentalist preachers. If you want to become a charismatic, then listen to charismatic preachers. If you want to become a liberal, then listen to liberal preachers, for sooner or later you will become that which influences you. You will not have the radio on to compromisers all day long and still become a strong, separated Christian.

The same is true concerning books. Many Christians become rabid followers of authors they have never met, of preachers whose churches they have never visited, and of men and women about whom they know nothing. They allow themselves to be unequally yoked with a personality that will influence them but about which they know little or nothing!

Let's go back to the original purpose of this chapter. First, we decide what we want to be. Then we find the influence that is like that and we position ourselves in its presence, in order that we may be influenced accordingly.

Years ago a young man heard me preach on several occasions. He decided he wanted to be the kind of preacher that Brother Hyles is, so he moved to Hammond. (At the time he was single.) When he got to our area, he then enrolled in a college whose philosophies basically are contrary to ours. The time spent in that college each week was far greater than the time spent under my influence, but he felt he could go to that college, choose what was good and leave the bad. He did not realize that no one can do this! There is no way that a person can disassociate himself from being influenced by his environment. This was the case. Years have passed. He is now a pastor with no desire at all to be like Brother Hyles.

The issue here is not that he should want to be or not want to be like Brother Hyles. The issue is that he wanted to be one thing and chose an environment that influenced him to be another.

7. *Have a degree of closeness to all church members.* This does not mean that you should be socially involved with all church members. It does mean, however, that within a church each member should have a positive feeling toward every other member. Instead of having a positive and a negative, have degrees of positive.

For example, I am an independent, fundamental Baptist. I certainly feel kindly toward all of that group. However, within that group there are different degrees of acceptance. There are some preachers within that group that I would have preach for me, I would preach for them, and I would preach with them. There are others within that group for whom I would preach and with whom I would preach, but I would not have preach for me. There are others in that group with whom I would preach, but I would not have them preach for me, nor would I preach for them. There are still others in that group whom I would not have preach for me, for whom I would not preach and with whom I would not preach, but I would certainly be willing to sit down and have a cup of tea and some warm fellowship with them. I do not feel negatively toward any of them, but there are degrees of my positive feeling.

Concerning fundamental colleges—there are numbers of colleges in America that I would consider fundamental. I am for them all, but I am more for some than for others. It may be that I would recommend a student to attend my first choice. If that student felt negative about that recommendation, I would then recommend my second choice, then my third, etc. This does not mean that my first choice is always the same. It may be that for one young person I would have a different first choice than for another.

Then there are other young people who I feel would not consider going to my first choice for them. I would be pleased and somewhat surprised to have them even choose my last choice among the colleges that are acceptable to me.

This is the way it should be in a church. The Bible says we are to love one another, to prefer one another, to forgive one another, to be kind to one another, and to be forbearing with one another.

8. *Then choose from the church a circle of companions and fellowship.* This circle should be composed of those who are already what you want yourself to become. While the Christian is supposed to love all fellow-Christians and fellow-church members, there are those in that group whom he should not choose as his closest associates and the crowd with whom he is going to run. A good rule of thumb is that you be in the minority when wanting to be helped and that you be in the majority when wanting to help. If there is a weak Christian whom you want to help, by all means be sure that you have other strong Christians that form the majority. You should be in the minority only when you yourself are trying to become strong, and therefore associate yourself with such a crowd.

So we have chosen a large circle, composed of all the church members about whom we are to feel positive. Then we have chosen a smaller circle with whom we are to be companions.

9. *Then choose an even smaller circle to whom you will be good friends.* Here are several observations about this small circle to whom you give your friendship:

1) *God must lead you in the choosing of those to whom you will be a friend.* This is a knitting done by God as was the case of Jonathan toward David. **I Samuel 18:1, "And it came to pass, when he had made an end of speaking unto Saul, that the soul of Jonathan was knit with the soul of David, and Jonathan loved him as his own soul."** God must lead you in becoming such a friend.

We are using the word "friend" here in the sense it is meant to be used. Occasionally someone will say, "She is a true friend." There is no other kind of friend. The word "friend" in the Bible is a very important and serious word. It is a relationship that is akin to brother, father, mother, sister, son, daughter. **Proverbs 18:24, "A man that hath friends must shew himself friendly: and there is a friend that sticketh closer than a brother." Proverbs 27:10, "Thine own friend, and thy father's friend, forsake not; neither go into thy brother's house in the day of thy calamity: for better is a neighbour that is near than a brother far off." Proverbs 17:17, "A friend loveth at all times, and a brother is born for adversity."**

2) *This friendship is for life.* You cannot lose a friend. There is no such statement that can be truthfully uttered as, "He was my friend," "I was his friend," "We used to be good friends." The wise man said that a friend loveth at all times.

3) *This friendship need not be returned.* Now to be sure, anyone who chooses to be the friend of another would prefer that that person also become his friend, but if it is Bible friendship, it need not be returned, and nothing can stop or quench it. It is best for the Christian to become the friend of another without expecting that friendship to be reciprocated or returned. Then there is no hurt that can come. The wise Christian will not allow the presence of happiness to be determined by others. He will, however, allow the degree of that happiness to be determined by others. This friendship is for life. If it is not returned, it is still alive. If its object becomes your enemy, you are still his friend.

Perhaps the true test of real friendship is, "Does it have to be returned?"

Many years ago God knitted my soul to that of Dr. John R. Rice. I became his friend. Now I never gave much thought as to whether he was my friend. I enjoyed every kindness that he ever sent my way and every gracious thing that he ever did for me, but that was not necessary. I was his friend. If he was my friend, wonderful. If not, my friendship would not be affected.

4) *You can be close to the one to whom you are a friend by*

*unilateral action; by that I mean, you may choose to be close to anyone to whom you want to be close.* The other person need not move toward you. (Of course, I am talking about heart closeness which, of course, is the best.) If I choose to get close to an object, there is nothing that object can do about it, and if I want in my heart to feel close to someone, I can do so. They need not even know about it. I can pray for them regularly, take time to love them in my heart, think of their burdens, and be compassionate toward them, and all of this will need no reciprocation whatsoever.

Recently I was in a distant state. When I finished preaching on Monday night, a pastor came and waited in line for about 30 minutes to talk to me. When his turn came, he sincerely and warmly looked me in the eye and told me that he loved me and that I had no idea how much. Now I did not even know the brother, but it was obvious that he loved me and that he felt close to me, and though to my knowledge I had never seen him, I somehow felt that he was my friend. So, no doubt there are some to whom I feel close who do not feel close to me. There are some who feel close to me whom I do not even know. Both do not have to move.

Often someone will say, "I just can't get close to him." Oh, yes, you can! What you are saying is that you can't get him to feel close to you, but you can come as close to him as you want. He cannot do a thing to prevent your love or your friendship.

5) *Retain a bit of formality even with your closest friends.* I have known personally and often intimately the greatest Christians of the last 100 years. I have noticed something very interesting. All of the great men retain a little mystique and a touch of formality even with their closest friends. For example, Dr. John R. Rice and Dr. Bob Jones, Sr. were very close friends, and I knew them both well. In spite of their close friendship, there was a bit of dignity in their manner toward each other. I have preached with them so many times I can almost hear their conversation, as follows:

"Hello, Dr. Bob. Nice to see you again."

"Hello, Dr. John. How's Mrs. Rice and the family?"

"They are well, thank you, and how's Mrs. Jones, and how's the work at the university doing?"

"We are having a good year, Dr. Rice. Is the Sword of the Lord doing well?"

Of course, they had their time of levity and warm expressions, but it was always seasoned with a refreshing touch of dignity and class.

I believe that this should exist even among family members. The word might be mystique. Any relationship, no matter how close, certainly should include propriety, manners, grace and kindness and gentleness.

This certainly should be manifest concerning one's person. The father who allows his children to see him around the house in his underclothing will not develop a proper relationship with his children. Even husbands and wives should take care to behave in the same manner. Our children, for example, have never seen their dad's bare feet. They have never seen me in my pajamas or underclothing. I feel very close to my children, and when they were at home we were all good buddies and very expressive of our love and closeness, but Dad was always Dad, and he always dressed like Dad. I always came to the table fully clothed. Bear in mind that I was more than their father; I was also their pastor, their school superintendent, and later on, their college chancellor.

Friendship is a wonderful relationship, but it should not be taken for granted, and certainly a friend should be treated with the same courtesy and grace that is offered to a casual acquaintance and even to a stranger.

So we have accepted all the members of the church family with a positive outlook, loving them all. This is the great wide circle. From that wide circle we have chosen a group that is a smaller circle with whom we fellowship, and from that smaller circle there is yet a much smaller circle of those to whom God has led us to be friends. I have often said, "Happy is a person who has a friend. Happier is the person who is a friend. Happiest is the person who has a friend and is a friend." What a relationship! Put it right up there beside the closest relationships of life—that relationship of friendship!

# Chapter 17

# The End Result of Improper Relationships

Hebrews 10:29, "Of how much sorer punishment, suppose ye, shall he be thought worthy, who hath trodden under foot the Son of God, and hath counted the blood of the covenant, wherewith he was sanctified, an unholy thing, and hath done despite unto the Spirit of grace?"

Acts 7:51, "Ye stiffnecked and uncircumcised in heart and ears, ye do always resist the Holy Ghost: as your fathers did, so do ye."

I Thessalonians 5:19, "Quench not the Spirit."

Ephesians 4:30, "And grieve not the holy Spirit of God, whereby ye are sealed unto the day of redemption."

The reader will be near the end of the chapter before fully realizing its purpose and its right to be in this book.

There are several sins against the Holy Spirit mentioned in the Bible. Four of these sins can be committed by the child of God.

1. *Insulting the Holy Spirit.* **Hebrews 10:29, "Of how much sorer punishment, suppose ye, shall he be thought worthy, who hath trodden under foot the Son of God, and hath counted the blood of the covenant, wherewith he was sanctified, an unholy thing, and hath done despite unto the Spirit of grace?"** "Insulting the Holy Spirit" simply means "to leave Him alone." This is the Christian who will not do what He says. To understand this Christian, you have to understand the book of Hebrews. The book

of Hebrews was written to Hebrew Christians. God is admonishing them not to neglect their salvation, but to continue growing in the grace and knowledge of our Lord Jesus. He likens the land of Egypt to the condition of the natural man. **I Corinthians 2:14, "But the natural man receiveth not the things of the Spirit of God: for they are foolishness unto him: neither can he know them, because they are spiritually discerned."** God compares the wilderness to the carnal Christian and the promised land to the Spirit-filled Christian. God is telling the person who has been saved, that he is out of Egypt and on his way to the promised land, going through the wilderness; he is to continue on into the promised land and live the Spirit-filled life. The Israelites are used as an example. They left the land of Egypt because of God's deliverance through the passover lamb. They went into the wilderness and across the wilderness as God led them. They came to the door of the promised land at Kadesh-barnea. They sent twelve spies to check out the promised land. They came back with glowing reports of its beauty and of its fruitfulness but told the people that they could not go in. The people decided not to go in, and because they made this decision, God sent them back into the wilderness and told them that not one adult would see or enter into the promised land, except Caleb and Joshua, who were the two spies who voted to go into the land. The people paid no attention to God's command. They had not listened to God's order, and in so doing, they committed the awful sin of insulting the Holy Spirit!

2. *Resisting the Holy Spirit.* **Acts 7:51, "Ye stiffnecked and uncircumcised in heart and ears, ye do always resist the Holy Ghost: as your fathers did, so do ye."** "Resisting" is the sin of listening to the Holy Spirit but disobeying Him. They did not insult Him, for they did give Him a hearing, but having heard, they refused to obey. However, this sin is committed before the previous one. Nobody insults the Holy Spirit by refusing to listen to Him until they have listened to Him and disobeyed. Ananias and Sapphira listened to Him and disobeyed. This is not as great a sin as insulting Him. It is on the road to insulting Him, and they never

would have insulted Him had they not resisted Him. In other words, if they had not refused to do what He said to do, they would never have gone on to refuse to listen. The order is: First, resist by listening and not doing, and then later, why listen? They didn't obey anyway.

3. *Quenching the Holy Spirit.* **I Thessalonians 5:19, "Quench not the Spirit."** This is the sin of listening, considering what He says, and obeying some of what He says and disobeying the rest. In other words, quenching is the screening of what the Holy Spirit says. The Christian hears the Holy Spirit and reads the Book the Holy Spirit authored. He gives serious consideration to obedience. In some areas he obeys; in some areas he disobeys. This is a terrible sin, but not as bad as resisting. Resisting is a terrible sin, but not as bad as insulting. It is better to listen to the Holy Spirit, consider what He says and do some of it than it is to listen to Him and reject. It is better to listen and reject than it is to refuse to listen. It is interesting to note this order: First, quenching—listening and screening, obeying some and disobeying some; second, resisting—listening and refusing; third, insulting—refusing to listen.

The quenching of the Holy Spirit is the condition of most Christians. We read the Bible, decide what sounds reasonable to us and obey that which is reasonable. We hear the preacher preach and screen what he says, decide what sounds logical to us and decide on that basis what to obey. The average Christian sits in the pew and quenches or screens the Holy Spirit. The average Christian reads the Bible and does likewise.

4. *Grieving the Holy Spirit.* **Ephesians 4:30, "And grieve not the holy Spirit of God, whereby ye are sealed unto the day of redemption."** Now notice what grieves Him. Very carefully read the verses adjacent to **Ephesians 4:30.** It grieves the Holy Spirit when His children do not get along with each other. It grieves Him when we fuss, when we fight. It grieves Him when we criticize each other. It grieves Him when His children are improperly related one to the other.

These sins are a downhill slide. First the Christian grieves the

Holy Spirit, then he quenches the Holy Spirit, then he resists the Holy Spirit, then he insults the Holy Spirit. If he can have the victory over resisting the Holy Spirit, he will not insult Him. If he can have the victory over quenching, he will not resist or insult Him. If he can have the victory over grieving the Holy Spirit, he will not quench Him or resist Him or insult Him. In other words, the first step down is grieving the Holy Spirit. After we grieve Him by being improperly related to God's people, we then begin to quench Him, by listening to Him but not accepting all He commands us to do. Once that is done, we continue downhill to resisting Him, which means that we listen to what He says but refuse to do it. Once that is done, we continue our downhill trek to come to the depth of the Christian sin against the Holy Spirit, that of insulting Him, or not listening at all.

This shows the importance of our proper treatment of God's people. This is why we ought to relate ourselves properly to the fallen, the weak, the strong, the brokenhearted and others in God's family. If somehow we could win the victory over grieving the Holy Spirit, we could certainly win the victory over quenching Him, resisting Him and insulting Him.

This means that the one who does the grieving is the loser. He grieves the Holy Spirit and because he does, he qualifies himself to quench the Holy Spirit, resist the Holy Spirit and insult the Holy Spirit, and soon the Christian life is wasted and rather useless. The one whom he hates is not the loser; the hater is the loser. The one who is the object of bitterness is not the loser; the bitter one is the loser. I have often said I would rather be the hated than the hater, the object of gossip rather than the gossiper, the rebuked rather than the rebuker.

Oh, people of God, let us not grieve the Holy Spirit by improper relationships with each other and bad attitudes toward each other.

The same is true in all of life's relationships. Ask any pastor. He looks out in the congregation and sees one of his members with "that look" on his face. Any pastor knows what I am talking about. It is that look of discontent, a look of uncooperativeness. Something is wrong between that person and the pastor or the church or something about the church program.

It isn't long until he begins to screen what is said from the pulpit. The pastor he once trusted, he no longer trusts. He begins to quench what is said from the pulpit. He screens what is preached. He no longer gives himself to the pastor. His loyalty is waning.

Then comes the next step. He has grieved, he has quenched, and now he resists. He listens to what the pastor says with no intention at all of responding. He now has a look of resistance on his face. Every pastor has seen it over and over again. The person listens with rebellion and resistance.

Then comes the last stage. He insults the pastor by not even listening. He pays him no mind at all. It is as if the pastor does not exist. The tragedy is that the member is the loser. Of course, the godly pastor is grieved and disappointed, but if he has the right attitude and the right love in his heart toward the member, he will not be damaged, except by disappointment.

Usually after the cycle is run, the disenchanted, then disgruntled, then rebellious church member goes somewhere else. He soon finds that the new pastor and the new church are not perfect either. He finds the same conditions there that embittered him before, and after a few months or years, the imperfections of the new pastor and church are discovered. Then comes the same disenchantment, followed by the quenching or the screening, followed by the listening but resisting, then followed by the insulting or not listening at all.

Not long ago I was talking to a pastor in the area. I asked him how a certain family was doing that at one time had been members of First Baptist Church of Hammond. They had gone through the aforementioned cycle and had left our church. When I asked the pastor how they were doing, he said, "Oh, they left our church a long time ago." Then he asked me about a couple who had come to our church from his after having gone through the cycle at his church. I replied that that couple had already come and gone at First Baptist Church and that they had left us also. This is not saying that every one who leaves a church goes through that cycle, but every man of God who has ever pastored a church knows what I am talking about. The people would not have refused to listen had they not first listened and resisted. They would not have listened and resisted had they not first quenched or screened the messages. They would not have quenched had they not become disenchanted with the pastor and/or church members.

The same thing is true with friends. A person becomes enchanted with another person and what is called a friendship is started. It is usually a fast and strong relationship, but soon the imperfections of the friend begin to show. Perhaps the parties got too close to each other. At any rate, there was some disappointment, followed by disenchantment, followed by quenching, followed by resisting, followed by an ignoring and the so-called friendship has been severed. Then there comes along another attractive personality, and the same cycle is followed again and again and again.

The secret is, do not be grieved. Don't take the first step down. The entire purpose of this chapter is to lead us to realize the destination of a trip that is started by improper relationships with our brothers and sisters in Christ. Don't get on the highway. Don't start the slide down. Keep your heart right with God's people. Not doing so is the initial sin a Christian can commit against the Holy Spirit. Once that sin is committed, the quenching follows. Once the quenching, then comes the resisting, followed by the insulting. The result is a hard, cold Christian who has arrived at a destination of which he had never thought and for which he had never planned. And to think—it all started because of improper treatment of fellow-Christians.

# Chapter 18

# The Principle of Waiting

**Isaiah 40:31, "But they that wait upon the Lord shall renew their strength; they shall mount up with wings as eagles, they shall run, and not be weary; and they shall walk, and not faint."**

One of the mst important qualities dealing with human relationships is the quality of waiting. There are times in our relationships when it is best to do nothing and wait. The wise Christian will discover these times.

1. *Act swiftly, but do not decide swiftly.* There is certainly nothing wrong with swift action, but let it not be hasty action. In other words, let us wait until the decision is clear, until the solution is obvious. Once this has come, let swift action follow.

2. *It is usually wise for the pastor to wait before giving marital counseling.* Most wounds heal themselves if left alone. If picked at, they can become infected. Most problems solve themselves, and many small problems become big problems because they are attacked too soon and picked at too often. I found, for example, that when a husband and wife contact me for marital counseling, it is best to wait two or three days before actually having the counseling session. Most of the problems will solve themselves or be solved by the couple within two or three days. A little wait is often wise.

3. *It is wise to wait before hiring employees.* Most pastors and churches hire too quickly. We become enchanted with someone

who has talent and ability and hire him before making a thorough investigation. A five-and-ten-cent-store clerk is usually investigated more carefully than is an assistant pastor, and sad to say, sometimes even more carefully than the pastor! No pastor in the world has a finer staff than do I, and no pastor in the world has had through the years finer people to work with him than has this preacher. I have never had a serious problem with a staff member, and certainly some of the finest men and women in the world are those who have worked for me and with me through these 40 years of pastoring. I am convinced that one reason for this record is that I wait carefully and watch carefully before hiring a staff member. This is especially true concerning assistant pastors and full-time male staff members. In some cases I have watched a man for three years or more before hiring him. In many cases, I have considered employing a man when at first I felt that he was the answer, and had a tremendous urge and desire to hire him immediately; however, I have always waited and have always been glad. In some cases, the time of waiting proved the man's integrity, value and loyalty. In other cases, waiting proved that the man was not what I believe God wanted. The same pastor who advises his young people to wait until they know someone before marriage will quickly hire a staff member in an hour or two with whom he wants to have a lifetime ministry!

4. *Wait before making a significant purchase.* Much of the financial problem in America has been caused by impulsive buying! We see it; we want it; we buy it! It is amazing how quickly we become disenchanted with most of our purchases. Such purchases as houses, cars, furnishings, appliances, and even clothing should not be made hastily.

Just yesterday I received a letter from a young lady who has grown up in our church. She is one of my favorites, and she is married to a fine young man who is a graduate of Hyles-Anderson College. In the note that she wrote me just yesterday, she told me about a piece of furniture that they had seen for which they had fallen, and which they were going to buy. Its price was $1200. They agreed to purchase it, but just before the purchase, the young man said to his wife, "You know, we have always taken Brother Hyles' advice, and Brother Hyles has advised us to wait before making large purchases in order to be sure that we are doing the right thing." What he was saying was the Brother Hyles has warned his people against compulsive buying! They agreed to wait, and during the waiting period, they found that neither of them thought it was wise to purchase the $1200 piece of furniture. Soon there came a letter of thanks to me in appreciation for this very truth that I have taught through these years in First Baptist Church.

5. *Wait before dismissing an employee.* Many churches have been seriously damaged because of a hasty dismissal of a staff member. In 40 years of pastoring, I have never "fired" a staff member. There have been times when I was tempted to do so, but I always waited and an answer always came. Sometimes the answer was to transfer the person to another area of the ministry. Sometimes the answer was to wait patiently, and on occasion the answer came when I felt that perhaps I myself was the problem and not the employee.

When someone is employed to work with me, the decision is a twofold one. It is a decision that I make and a decision that he makes. Now if later I find that it was a mistake, is it fair for only one of us to suffer when both of us sinned? I think not. Since the decision for his coming to work with me was mine as well as his, and in most cases it was a decision that I made first, for I had approached him about coming to work with me, I have found it difficult in light of this fact to dismiss an employee quickly. Shall he suffer, his wife suffer, his children suffer because he and I shared in a mistake that was first my idea?

Suppose with me for a moment that I dismiss an assistant pastor or another male staff member. Notice all the losses that are incurred. He loses his job, he loses his church, he loses his pastor, he loses his friends, he loses his house, he loses his office, he loses his work. His wife loses her house, her kitchen, her Sunday school class, her friends, her church and her pastor. His children lose their school, their house, their room, their friends, their Sunday school class, their Sunday school teacher, their pastor and many other things. What do I lose? I lose nothing, and if I want him to leave, I actually gain. So because of an action that I initiated and in which I shared equally, I gain and everybody else loses. Most of these unfortunate occurrences can be prevented by the simple act of waiting before hiring and, yes, waiting before firing!

6. *Wait before spanking a child.* Most of our disciplining of children is simply the parent throwing a temper tantrum because the child threw a temper tantrum. Add to this the fact that no person should ever spank a child in the heat of passion and anger, and you will be led to wait before spanking a child. As our children were growing up, I always spanked them in the privacy of their rooms. I did not spank them in the presence of other family members or guests in our home. When the crime was committed, I simply told the child to go to her room. She would go there and wait for me, and I would wait before inflicting the punishment. I wanted to be sure that I was doing the right thing, and I wanted to be sure that I was not punishing under the emotion of anger or temper. After I was convinced that the thing to do was to spank the child, and after I had calmed down sufficiently to do it in love, I went to the room where the child was waiting, I sat down beside her on the bed, told her that I loved her and asked her if she knew what she did that was wrong. She explained to me what infraction she had committed, and then I explained to her that God had told me in the Bible I was supposed to spank her. I explained that I did not want to, but that I had to, and that it was not because I was angry but because I wanted her to grow up to be the right kind of person. I then asked her to bend over my knee, and I spanked her. Following the spanking, I prayed for God to bless her, and I thanked Him for her. Then I assured her of my love and suggested that she stay in the room for awhile to think about what she had done. I left the room and usually returned in about five minutes. I hugged her, kissed her and told her she could leave her room.

I did not tell her when she was sent to her room that I was going to spank her. I simply said, "Go to your room." If I told her I was going to spank her and then felt later that I was making a mistake, I would have broken my word, so I simply sent her to her room to wait. This waiting time was for Daddy more than for daughter—a time for me to decide what course of action to take and a time for me to prepare to take that course of action in the right spirit and with the right attitude.

7. *Wait before accepting a resignation.* Through 40 years of pastoring I have found wisdom in asking people to wait before finalizing the decision to resign. This applies to any office of the church, whether paid or volunteer. Many people resign under the emotion of anger, discouragement, weariness or any one of many other emotions. I almost always ask the person to do me a favor and wait for 30 days before finalizing his decision to resign. Perhaps the anger will have subsided, the body will be stronger, the illness will be cured or the discouragement will be passed within the 30-day waiting period. I do not beg them to stay unless I feel very, very strongly that they are leaving the will of God, but I do ask them to wait for 30 days. At least half of the time their minds have changed, which means that they would have been disappointed had they been allowed to resign immediately.

8. *Wait before giving a resignation.* The wise person will not submit a resignation immediately upon feeling that he should do so. He should give himself at least 30 days before resigning. I do not mean that he should resign and give a 30-day notice. I mean that he should give himself a 30-day notice before resigning, and no one but he himself should be aware of the decision that he is considering. Many employers are so wounded when they find that an employee is considering leaving that the wound of disappointment is never healed, even though the employee remains.

I have a dear friend who many years ago was pastoring a church. He was being blessed of God in a wonderful way and had one of the fastest growing churches in our area. One Sunday morning the song leader was late, the pianist hadn't arrived, and it seemed like everything that could go wrong did go wrong! He got up in the pulpit, he was discouraged and a bit angry, and simply announced that next Sunday would be his last Sunday! Next Sunday was his last Sunday, but he has never had the ministry anywhere else that he had there. He left something at that church, and I am convinced that he believes he made the mistake of his lifetime. No one should ever resign under emotion.

I have a sermon that I have preached a time or two entitled, "Don't Make a Decision When Your Decision-Maker Is Broken." Most of life's biggest decisions are made without a sound decision-maker. A decision affecting one's life should never be made when discouraged, sick, defeated, lonely, sad, angry, etc. Wait until the decision-maker is fixed before making the decision, and if the decision must be made before the decision-maker is repaired, take the decision to someone who has a good sound decision-maker and have that person make the decision for you.

9. *Wait before mailing a letter of rebuttal.* All of us have become angered because of an unkind letter and have responded with an unkind answer. We have failed to remember that a soft answer turneth away wrath. We have answered hastily and angrily only to wish later that we could retrieve the letter, but it is too late. The letter is gone. Through these years I have written many such letters myself, but it has been my policy to write them immediately but wait at least seven days before mailing them. Most of them are never mailed, and my desire to have that letter back can be granted. Of course, if one could wait seven days to write the letter, he would be even wiser, but most of us want to write it now! If this is the case, give it to someone whom you trust, seal it so they cannot read it, and ask them to hold it for you for seven days. After seven days, go get it and then decide, without emotion of any kind, whether it is wise to mail it. Upon rare occasions, after seven days have passed, I go ahead and mail the letter. On other occasions, I tear it up and then sometimes I dispose of it and write another that is kind and conciliatory.

10. *Wait before making a verbal rebuttal.* The old saying of, "Count to ten before answering," is still a wise one. A word cannot

be retrieved. You can write a letter and hold it before mailing; you cannot do that with a word. It is forever gone, has forever done its damage, and can never be retrieved! Because of this, every Christian should develop the habit of waiting before answering if it is a rebuttal that he is making. Oh, the words that we have said that we would love to retrieve, but that is impossible. All of the "I'm sorry's" and "Forgive me's" cannot retract a word said in haste.

Someone asked me at a question-answer session recently what changes I would make if I had my life to live over. I immediately replied that I would like to have an opportunity to relive times when I had said some things I shouldn't have said. The wise Christian will oftentimes say such things as, "Give me a chance to think about that for awhile," or "Let me chew on that for a little while." May God teach us to wait!

11. *Wait before disagreeing with your mate.* If there is a disagreement, there is no law that requires you to make it known. It is not always completely necessary that you express your opinion. The wise husband, for example, will not make a rebuttal in disagreement with his wife, and 90% of the time would be wise not to even express his opinion if it is contrary to hers. She should be allowed to have opinions, activities and friends of her own. Thousands of hours of grief could be avoided if family members just realized that most of the times they needlessly express opinions and that they need not conform miscellaneous opinions with each other. If we could just learn not to speak but to wait!

12. *Wait before fighting.* This is true in the church, the home or the business. Most battles could be avoided if they were preceded by a waiting period. Thousands of churches have been divided because of hasty battles. Thousands of relationships have been damaged because of quick confrontations. Elsewhere in this manuscript it has been mentioned that a wonderful little slogan would be, "No attack; no defense." Perhaps we could add to that, "In case of disagreement, no expression of opinion." Much heartache has come to many people because at times of idle talk there is disagreement on some little insignificant issue. Wait. Be quiet. Make no

rebuttal. If there is something that you should say, you will still be able to say it later. The words that you use so quickly will still be understandable after you have waited awhile.

13. *Wait before borrowing money or before building.* This applies to a business, to a home, and especially to a church. That new shiny building that you covet may be your biggest enemy, especially if you are meeting in it and wondering how you are going to pay for it. Most churches spend their happiest years in small inadequate facilities. The journey is more fun than the destination, and once the church has arrived, it often loses something for which it would gladly trade its new building. Now the pastor may come to the people and ask them to follow him, and they may be willing to do so, but a long time before he comes to the people, he should have prayed, meditated, planned, thought, and yes, waited.

14. *Wait before making a decision.* Especially is this true concerning a decision of any magnitude. Take your time. Let the decision-making process cover most of your emotions in life. A hasty decision is usually a wrong decision; and if the hasty decision is the right decision, the door will still be open to make that decision after you have waited awhile.

For seven months I wrestled with the possibility of coming to Hammond. I can recall going into the children's bedrooms while they were asleep, getting on my knees and begging God not to let me make a mistake. I reminded God that the selection of their mates would depend on the decision that I was facing. Their schools, their friends and probably their life's work was in the balance. I felt that I simply could not make a hasty decision, so for seven months I wrestled, prayed, thought, cried, meditated and agonized!

When the decision was made, I did not change my mind. The truth is that there were times between the time I resigned the Miller Road Baptist Church in Garland, Texas, and the time that I left that I felt I had made a mistake, but I had made my decision over a period of seven months. I could not undo in doubt what I had done in faith, and I could not undo hastily what I had done carefully. Just as I had not made the decision to leave hastily, I should not hastily make the decision to change my mind. Again I say, wait!

15. *Wait before allowing your mind to condemn people who have left your fellowship.* It is easy to criticize hastily the people who leave your church. To be quite frank with you, I have never understood how people could share with a church and pastor years of blessing, sorrows, joys, victories, defeats, tears and laughter and then leave! It is totally beyond my comprehension! But it DOES happen, and when it does, the Christian spirit is to still love the people who have disappointed you. Look upon them as being alumni that are welcome to come back home to visit. Do not allow yourself to become bitter or wounded. Look upon them as you would look upon a son or daughter who has left home to go to college or into military service or to marry. Love them as you always loved them. If they do not love you, that doesn't keep you from being able to love them.

I have heard some preachers talk about the "back door revival" that they had. They often say it was the best thing that ever happened to the church. Well, if it was the best thing, it certainly was not the best thing for you to say it was the best thing! I have heard preachers say concerning members who left their church, "Good riddance; bad rubbish." I have never believed that, nor do I believe it now, and I pray God never to let me succomb to the temptation of having anything but love for people with whom I have served and whom I have loved through the years. Again, you will be glad if you simply wait before passing judgment.

16. *Wait before giving your opinion, even when asked.* Of course, as we mentioned elsewhere, it is usually wise not to give an opinion unless asked, but even when asked, it is usually wise to wait before giving an opinion. Often I say when asked for advice, "Let me think on that awhile," "Let me pray about that for awhile," "Let me meditate about that for awhile," or "Give me a few days to think about it." As a pastor, I am often asked to advise people concerning decisions that affect many lives and entire lives. I constantly feel the weight of responsibility on my shoulders and

constantly plead with God for wisdom to give the advice that Jesus would give. There are many times when I feel before such advice is given there must be a time of waiting.

17. *In a church, wait before starting a new ministry.* Now this wait is somewhat different from the others. For example, a pastor and church can become enchanted with a particular ministry such as starting a class for Spanish-speaking people. This can be so exciting to them as they look forward to it that they can too hastily choose the leader. I found it wise to let the right leader determine the ministry that is started. I wait before I start a ministry until God sends the right leader who has a burden for that ministry.

I was Pastor of the First Baptist Church of Hammond for 11 years before I started a school. For some time I felt I should start such a ministry, but I felt that I should wait until the time was right.

Some pastors make unwise decisions to start bus ministries too soon. Others start schools too soon, and in so doing, time is used for these ministries that should be used for the regular work of the church, and many churches have been damaged because ministries were started before waiting.

Let me say a word of warning to church members. This advice is not being given to you to cause you to start trouble in the church. If the pastor has waited and then presents the program, it is almost always best for you to go along with him, and even if you do not go along with him, it is never wise to cause trouble! Follow God's man! Moses waited a long time before he led the children of Israel out of Egypt, but they did not know he was waiting. To them it may have appeared to be a hasty decision, but to Moses it was after a time of waiting. Paul appeared to be a bit impetuous in many of his decisions, but he had waited three years in the deserts of Arabia. Again I say, wait.

Jesus said to the apostles, "Tarry ye in Jerusalem." The prophet Isaiah reminded us to wait upon the Lord. Jesus admonished us concerning His return to watch and wait.

Wait until you are sure, and be sure to wait! When a solid assurance comes to act and when this assurance comes after a period of waiting, make haste to implement the work that God has led you to do and the thing that God has called you to do. Let not the waiting be done concerning the work which you know you are to do. Let the waiting be done in making the decision that it is His will that the work be done!

# Chapter 19

# Dying for Fellow Christians

I Corinthians 15:31, "I protest by your rejoicing which I have in Christ Jesus our Lord, I die daily."

Romans 8:36, "As it is written, For thy sake we are killed all the day long; we are accounted as sheep for the slaughter."

Galatians 2:20, "I am crucified with Christ: nevertheless I live; yet not I, but Christ liveth in me: and the life which I now live in the flesh I live by the faith of the Son of God, Who loved me, and gave Himself for me."

I love the woods! I spend much of my time alone with God in them. I have a little place in the woods where I go daily just for the purpose of praising God. I spend 15 minutes at that sacred little spot. For 60 seconds I write on a card or a paper the things that God has done for me recently. After I have made the list, I then go back through the list and praise God for each of them. It is not unusual for me to clap my hands, even take off my shoes and have a little spell as I praise God for what He has done for me.

I then leave that little spot in the woods and go to another. Though the branches at the first spot seem to clap themselves together when I arrive for my praise time, the branches at the second spot seem to bow themselves reverently, because this is where I go to worship. I take 60 seconds to list the things that God is, such as, God is merciful, God is gracious, God is longsuffering, God is forbearing, God is love. Then I go back through the list of what God is and worship Him for what He is. I spend 15 minutes at this worship place.

I then go to another little place in the woods where I confess my sins. This is done beneath a weeping willow tree, because I do not want to be the only one weeping when I confess. I begin by taking about 60 seconds and listing my sins. Then I go back through the list and plead for forgiveness and strength over temptation. I do this for about 15 minutes.

Then I go to a little place in the woods that is the most sacred of all. It is a place where I pray and present my petitions to God. It is where I plead for power. It is where I plead for His mercy, His guidance, His leadership. It is here where I pray for each member of my family by name and ask God's blessings upon them. This is my prayer place and the fourth stop in my daily journey through the woods. I usually spend a minimum of an hour at this place. One day a week I spend about 3 hours there and still another day a week I spend from 4 to 5½ hours there. Because of this, the woods are very dear to me.

My favorite time of the year in the woods is the wintertime, while the trees are bare. The reason this is my favorite season is that this is the time when the trees are alive. This is not the usual opinion. Most people would say that the trees are alive in the spring and the summer, but quite to the contrary! The trees are dying in the spring, the summer and the fall. They are alive in the winter. This is when life is coming into them that will be spent in the spring and summer and finally in the fall, so the trees are living while the branches are bare. New life is entering. The trees are dying when covered with leaves, for then the life is being spent.

Each evening I take my cordless electric shaver and plug it into the wall socket. Through the night it is being charged. It is living. Life is entering. Then I take it with me the next day and use it. While it is being used, it is dying. It is using up the life that it got through the night. This is the way the trees are. They are living in the wintertime as they gather life. They are dying in the spring, summer and fall as they are giving up that life.

This is what Paul meant when he said in **Romans 8:36, "For thy sake we are killed all the day long."** Notice it is "all the DAY long." He tells us why he is killed all the day long. It is for the sake of God's people.

Now read **I Corinthians 15:31, "I protest by your rejoicing which I have in Christ Jesus our Lord, I die daily."** Notice especially the three words, "I die daily." Give special attention to the word DAILY. Actually he is saying, "I serve daily," because serving is dying. Living is time spent with God when new life is received. Dying is time spent with our fellow-Christians in service to them and for them. Paul could not say that he died daily if he had not spent time living daily. So really what we think is death is life, and what we think is life is death. Paul wrote to Timothy and said, **"But she that liveth in pleasure is dead while she liveth."** John wrote the church at Sardis to tell them that they had a name that they were alive, but they were dead. What man thinks is life is death, and what man thinks is death is life! Death is the expenditure of life that is received while alone with God.

So the Christian life really has two major parts—living and dying. The living part is that time when we are plugged into Heaven. Dying is that time when we serve our fellowman as we expend the life we received while we were plugged into Heaven.

Hence, there are two tragedies in the Christian life. Some try to die all the time, but it doesn't work. Only that which is alive can die, and until a person is alive in Christ by communion with Him, he has no death to die. This is the reason for our futility in service for God. This is the reason for our powerless Christian lives. We go, go, go, serve, serve, serve, work, work, work, but we cannot die because we have no life to give. It is just routine with no blessing from Heaven and no power of God.

Another tragedy is the person who spends all of his time living. He never dies. He becomes so enchanted with the prayer closet and with the study that he spends all his time being plugged in and becomes much like a monk in a monastery. He is of no value to his fellowman because he is not willing to die. He gets to the place where he enjoys living so much that he refuses to go out into the highways and hedges to die for others.

The balanced Christian life is that life that spends hours alone with God living, then leaves the prayer closet and study to spend hours with man dying. To leave off the living means there is nothing that can die. To leave off the dying nullifies the purpose for living. What value is it if the tree receives life all winter only to refuse to give fruit, blossoms and leaves in the spring and summer and fall. On the other hand, the tree that receives no life will have nothing to die, and there can be no foliage.

One of the main reasons why Christian people cannot get along with each other is that we cannot die for each other or that we refuse to do so. Either we have no life to die for others because we have not spent time with God in securing a life to give, or we spend so much time securing life that we refuse to die for others, and they go unloved and unserved.

Yes, I love the woods. I love them in the spring when life springs forth and begins to die. I love them in the summer as they spend the life they gathered in the winter. I love them in the autumn when they are the most beautiful of all in death, and the dying process that started at birth is completed. I love them most in the wintertime, for though they lack the beauty and luster of the spring, summer and fall, nevertheless, I am aware that they are living and gaining life in order that they may die for us when spring comes.

Everything is born dying. When a baby is born, what really happens is that death is born. As soon as the cord is cut, the baby begins to die. They die at birth, or at least they begin to die at birth. What we want to do as human beings is postpone death as long as possible. We know that death is inevitable, but through diet, exercise, medicine, etc. we are trying to prolong the inevitable as long as possible. This is true with institutions. I am aware that someday Hyles-Anderson College will be in the hands of liberals, and I am aware that it is now dying. However, there are ways that that death can be prolonged and that its usefulness may continue for a longer period of time when it would without nurture and care.

May God help me to go to Him that I might live and go to others that I might die, and then go to Him that I might live and go to others that I might die. May I walk with Him in such a close communion that I will have a life to die for my brothers and sisters in Christ. May God help you, dear reader, to abide in Him that you may live and to spend that life dying for others. This is why Paul could write in **Galatians 2:20a, "I am crucified with Christ: nevertheless I live."** He lived and died and lived and died and lived and died. If there is no living, there is nothing to die, and if there is no dying, then there is no purpose in living. As the old man 88 years of age said on his deathbed as I held his bony hand, "Thank you, Preacher, for walking with God six days a week and for telling me on the seventh what God said."